Bible Arts & Crafts

Author: Kathryn Nider Wolf
Interior Design: Barry Slate
Cover: Kathryn Cole
Editor: Annie Galvin Teich

Pflaum Publishing Group
2621 Dryden Road, Suite 300
Dayton, OH 45439
800-543-4383
www.pflaum.com

ISBN 1-933178-35-3

Table of Contents

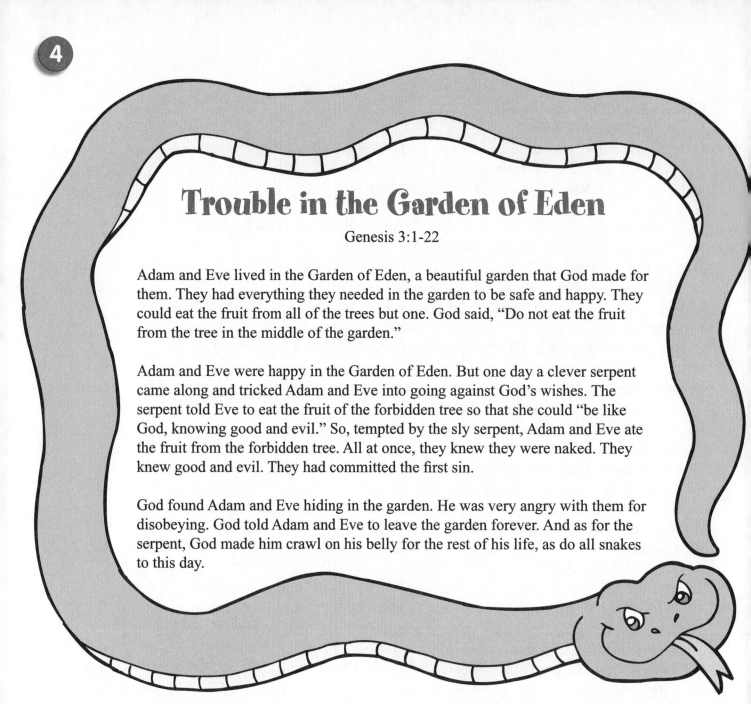

Trouble in the Garden of Eden

Genesis 3:1-22

Adam and Eve lived in the Garden of Eden, a beautiful garden that God made for them. They had everything they needed in the garden to be safe and happy. They could eat the fruit from all of the trees but one. God said, "Do not eat the fruit from the tree in the middle of the garden."

Adam and Eve were happy in the Garden of Eden. But one day a clever serpent came along and tricked Adam and Eve into going against God's wishes. The serpent told Eve to eat the fruit of the forbidden tree so that she could "be like God, knowing good and evil." So, tempted by the sly serpent, Adam and Eve ate the fruit from the forbidden tree. All at once, they knew they were naked. They knew good and evil. They had committed the first sin.

God found Adam and Eve hiding in the garden. He was very angry with them for disobeying. God told Adam and Eve to leave the garden forever. And as for the serpent, God made him crawl on his belly for the rest of his life, as do all snakes to this day.

Teacher Notes:
From boa constrictors to rattlesnakes, these creepy, crawly creatures fascinate children! Before telling the Bible story, show photos of different snakes and have children compare them. Identify the kinds of snakes and introduce children to the word *serpent*. Discuss how snakes move, what and how they eat, how they smell and catch their prey. If possible, have children feel a sample of snakeskin and describe it. Preschoolers will have fun pretending to slither on their bellies and move like snakes to music.

A Coiled Serpent

Objectives:

- Children should learn new vocabulary words such as *serpent, boa constrictor, slither, coil, poisonous, prey, venom, rattlesnake,* and *cobra.*
- Children should understand that snakes have been portrayed in stories as evil or bad, but that snakes are God's creatures too.
- Children can use their fine motor skills to sponge paint and cut out coiled snakes as reminders of the Bible story.

Materials: photos of real snakes, scissors, colored construction paper circle **or** one 9-in. paper plate per student, colored tempera paints in shallow dishes, sponges, hole punch, string or yarn, colored markers, ½-in. strip of red construction paper per child, glue sticks or school glue

Preparation: Reproduce the serpent pattern on page 80 on colored construction paper for each child **or** give each child a 9-in. paper plate.

Procedure:

1. Display the photos of real snakes and discuss their appearance, how they move and what they eat. Ask, "Who likes snakes? Why are some people afraid of snakes?" Have children recall why God made the serpent to crawl on its belly. Tell children they will be making a serpent to remind them of the trouble in the Garden of Eden.

2. Provide one pattern or paper plate per child. Demonstrate how to cut inward, around the circle, to produce a coiled snake.

3. Demonstrate how to sponge paint the circle in contrasting colors. Allow each child to cut out and paint his circle. Allow time to dry.

4. Have each child cut a V-shaped notch in one end of the strip of red construction paper, and then glue the strip, as shown, for the serpent's tongue.

5. Have children use markers to draw eyes.

6. Help young children to punch a hole in each serpent's head. Tie a length of string or yarn to hang the serpent from the ceiling. (Children may wish to name their snakes and write the chapter and verse on the back before taking them home.)

Cloudy With a Chance of Rain

Genesis 6:9-22; 7:1-9

The forecast was for forty days and forty nights of rain – not just a drizzle or a shower, but a downpour like no other thunderstorm before. In fact, it would be a *deluge* that would flood all the earth. But Noah was ready for the flood because he listened to God.

God told Noah to build a huge wooden boat and to gather two of every kind of animal on board. Noah's neighbors must have thought he was crazy, but Noah believed God and built the ark anyway. Noah and his family herded the animals on board, two-by-two, and they all waited for the storm. The thunder rolled and the lightning flashed. The rains came. Would the boat float?

Teacher Notes:

Young children will enjoy discovering what objects sink or float and then finger painting thunderclouds and lightning. After reading the story of Noah, have children share their experiences with heavy rain or thunderstorms. Provide young children with a tub of water and several items such as a plastic container, an apple, a lemon, a sponge, a rock, a metal spoon, and a piece of wood. Before placing each item in the water, ask, "Do you think this will sink or float?" To conclude, explain that God knew Noah's ark would float and it saved Noah, his family, and the animals on board.

Older children can compare types of rainfall and brainstorm words to describe kinds of rainfall such as *drizzle, shower, thunderstorm, downpour, hurricane, typhoon*, and *deluge*. Ask, "Where does all the rainwater go?" Older children can understand the concept of flooding and erosion. Have them create the flood scene with a resist technique of watercolors painted over crayon drawings.

The Great Flood Crayon Resist

Objectives:
- Children can use their fine motor skills to paint to sounds of rain using a new crayon resist technique.
- Older children can compare kinds of rain and discuss the effects of flooding and erosion.
- Young children will be able to express their feelings about thunder and lightning.

Materials: black, blue, and green watercolor paints; 9 in. x 12 in. glossy paper; crayons; one-inch paint brushes; newspaper to cover tables; sponges and paper towels for cleanup; pencil; tape recorder or CD player; recorded sounds of rainfall or a thunderstorm

Preparation: Prepare tables by spreading newspaper. Have the CD or tape player and recorded sounds ready to play.

Procedure:
1. Play the recorded sounds and have children tell about a thunderstorm they have experienced. Ask young children, "How did it make you feel?" Tell children they will paint rain and flashes of lightning.

2. Provide crayons, watercolors, and brushes at each table. Provide each child with a piece of glossy paper. Use the pencil to write each child's name on the back of his paper.

3. Have children use crayons to illustrate the ark, the rising floodwaters, and floating debris. Demonstrate how to apply the crayon with heavy strokes. Use white crayon to illustrate lightning with zigzag lines. Demonstrate how to use the wide brushes to apply a wash of black or blue watercolor paint. Remind students that the crayon will resist the wash of watercolor paints.

4. Then have students apply watercolor paint of their choice over their crayon drawings. As they are working, have children describe the rain and discuss the effects of flooding and erosion.

5. Allow pictures to dry and ask children to share their drawings and retell the story. Display paintings on a bulletin board entitled, "The Great Flood."

Genisis 7:1

God Sends a Sign

Genesis 7:1-14; 9:12-17

Just as God had promised, the ark floated, and Noah and his family were saved from the flood. When the rains stopped, they discovered that their huge boat had landed on the top of a mountain. Although the animals were restless, Noah waited as the floodwaters receded. Then he sent out a dove to look for dry land, but the dove returned. He waited seven more days and sent out another dove. This time the dove returned with an olive leaf. Noah waited a while longer before leaving the ark. When all was safe, God sent a rainbow as a sign and a promise that he would never again destroy the earth.

Teacher Notes:
Young children can identify the animals in a box of animal cookies and create animal pairs to tuck into their own personal Noah's ark to take home. Make sure you have plenty of animal cookies available for eating while they work!

Older children can learn the names of the colors of the rainbow in order by using the acronym ROY G. BIV to help them remember the sequence: red, orange, yellow, green, blue, indigo, and violet.

Noah's Ark Mobile

Objectives:
- Children will use their fine motor skills to color a rainbow with crayons and assemble a mobile.
- Children will be able to identify and sort animal cookies to create pairs.
- Children will remember the rainbow as a promise from God.

Materials: picture of a rainbow; box of animal cookies; precut ½ paper plate per child; ark pattern on page 81; 9 in. x 12 in. yellow or brown tag board; pencils, colored markers, or crayons; stapler; precut 24-in. length of yarn per child; one zippered plastic bag per child

Preparation: Precut ½ paper plate per child. Duplicate the ark pattern on page 81 to make several templates for children to trace.

Procedure:

1. Show the picture of the rainbow and ask children to name the colors in order: red, orange, yellow, green, blue, indigo, and violet. Ask, "Why did God send a rainbow?"

2. Provide each child with ½ paper plate and crayons. Demonstrate how to color the outside edge of the semicircle to create a rainbow. Allow children to color their rainbows and to color the center of the paper plate yellow.

3. Give each child a piece of tag board to fold in half as shown. Provide the ark template for children to place on the fold and trace. Make sure that the bottom of the ark is on the fold. Demonstrate how to cut through the folded tag board. Have each child cut, then staple on two sides to create a folded pocket.

4. Each child uses crayon or markers to write Noah's Ark and Genesis 7:1 on the front and to write his name on the back of the ark.

5. Glue the rainbow inside the open edge of the ark pocket as shown.

6. Help each child punch a hole at the top of the rainbow and attach a length of yarn to each mobile.

7. Give each child a zippered plastic bag. Tell children they will be selecting animals to put in their ark. Have children identify and sort five or six pairs of animal cookies each and place the cookies in plastic bags. Have students tuck their bags of animal cookies inside their arks to take home.

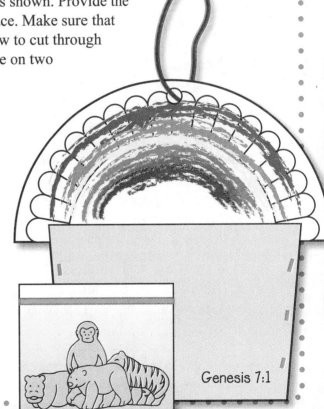

Genesis 7:1

Joseph and His Jealous Brothers

Genesis 37, 42-45

Jacob had twelve sons, but Joseph, his youngest son, was his favorite. One day the loving father gave Joseph a beautiful new robe of many colors. Joseph's brothers were jealous of all the special attention he got. They didn't like his boastful attitude either. In fact, they hated Joseph so much that they wanted to kill him. One brother, Reuben, tried to save Joseph. He suggested the brothers grab Joseph and throw him into a deep pit instead of killing him. Imagine how scared Joseph was in the bottom of that pit! What was going to happen to him?

The brothers decided to sell Joseph as a slave to some traders passing by on their way to Egypt. Joseph wouldn't be dead, but he would be out of the family and far away. They took Joseph's robe and covered it with goat's blood and told Jacob that a wild animal had eaten his son. Imagine how sad Jacob was when he heard his youngest son was dead!

Many years later, Jacob sent ten of his sons to Egypt to buy grain because his people were hungry. The brothers didn't know it, but Joseph had grown up to become the governor of the land. When they bowed down to him and asked to buy food, Joseph recognized his brothers. He was angry and called them spies. But Joseph could not stay mad at his brothers. Instead, he forgave them. Joseph realized that God had sent him ahead to help his people. Joseph hugged his brothers and told them to bring his father and his whole family to Egypt to live. So they did and Jacob had his sons together again.

Teacher Notes:
Young children will find this Bible story a little scary so focus on how much Jacob loved his son. Help children to see that feelings of anger and jealousy toward brothers and sisters are common, especially when a new baby arrives.

Older children can re-enact the story. Discuss sibling rivalry and feelings of jealousy. Ask them to think of times when they felt that a sibling got special attention or when they were jealous of another child. Emphasize that we never want to intentionally hurt our brothers and sisters and can forgive them when we are hurt.

Joseph's Robe Bag Puppet

Objectives:
- Children will cut and paste to make a paper bag puppet of Joseph in his coat of many colors.
- Children will identify feelings of jealousy, fear, sadness, and forgiveness and express feelings about their siblings.

Materials: one brown lunch bag per child; 1 in. x 9 in. colored construction paper strips; head, arms, and feet patterns reproduced on white paper for each child; scissors; brown or black yarn; school glue or glue sticks; crayons; slips of paper labeled with feelings

Preparation: Reproduce the patterns on page 82 on white paper for each child.

Procedure:

1. Provide the pattern page and scissors for each child to color and cut out the pieces.

2. Have each child use crayons to draw the eyes, nose, and mouth features and to color the face, arms, and feet.

3. Give each child a brown paper lunch bag. Demonstrate how to glue the sleeves of the coat to the front of the bag as shown.

4. Have each child overlap and glue the paper strips lengthwise on the front of each bag from the fold up.

5. Have each child open his bag to stand up, and then glue on the head, arms and feet as shown. Children may cut and glue yarn to add hair.

6. Distribute the feelings cards for the children to place inside the bag puppets to take home and discuss with parents.

Baby Moses Is Found in the Nile

Exodus 2:3–10

When Moses was born in Egypt, the Hebrews had been slaves for many years. A new king or Pharaoh ordered that all Hebrew baby boys were to be killed. To keep her baby safe, the mother of Moses hid him for three months. Then she put him in a basket made of papyrus reeds sealed with tar and placed the basket in the Nile River. Moses' sister Miriam waited and watched from the riverbank. What would happen to her baby brother?

As Miriam looked on, Pharaoh's daughter spotted the basket in the tall reeds along the riverbank. When the princess opened the basket, she saw the crying baby. She took pity and picked him up. "This must be one of the Hebrew babies," she said. Then Miriam came forward and asked, "Can I find a Hebrew woman to nurse the baby for you?" The princess agreed and the baby was returned to his mother. At the age of three, the boy was taken to live in the palace, and the princess raised him as her son. He was called Moses, which means drawn from the water.

Teacher Notes:
Young children can act out the story and pretend to find the baby Moses in the river. Provide a large basket with a baby doll wrapped in a blanket and a crown for the Egyptian princess.

Older children will be interested in basket weaving materials. If possible, bring in samples and discuss how baskets were used in ancient times to carry and store items. Baskets were also waterproofed to float and serve food.

A Baby in a Basket

Objectives:
- Children create "baskets" and Baby Moses figures.
- Children can use their basket replicas to retell the story of how Baby Moses was saved from the river.

Materials: two 6-in., white paper bowls per child; crayons; hole punch; yarn; scissors; one white paper napkin per child; black marker; pencils; white paper scraps; samples of woven baskets

Preparation: Precut two 4-in. lengths of yarn per child to tie the lid to the basket. Prepunch two holes two inches apart in the rim of each bowl.

Procedure:

1. Have children recall who found Baby Moses in the Nile. Ask, "How was the basket able to float?" Show sample baskets and describe how Moses' basket was made of papyrus reeds and coated with a sticky waterproof tar. Tell children they will make baskets for Baby Moses.

2. Provide two 6-in. paper bowls per child. Have children color the outside of their bowls with crayons if desired.

3. Give each child two pieces of yarn. Demonstrate how to tie the bowls together so that one bowl becomes a lid. Help younger children as needed.

4. Demonstrate how to fold the paper napkin as shown. Each child folds one corner of his napkin up as shown and then brings the two corners in to create a baby blanket. Have children secure the flaps with a dot of glue.

5. Have each child cut out a circle for the baby's head, draw on a face with crayons, and glue the baby's face above the fold as shown.

6. Each child places his Baby Moses in his basket to retell the story at home.

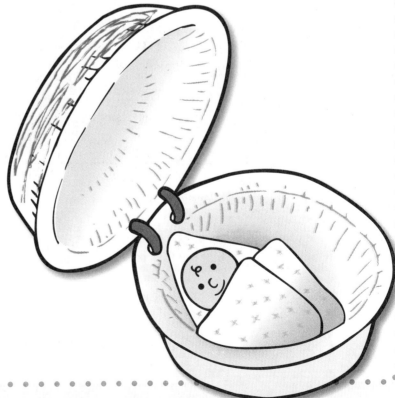

God Talks to Moses

Exodus 3-4

One day when Moses was tending a flock of sheep on the dry open range, a bright light caught his eye. Was it a campfire? Was it a forest fire? As Moses got closer, he saw that it was a bush that appeared to be on fire, but it didn't burn up. A voice spoke to Moses from inside the burning bush. The voice said, "Don't come any closer. Take off your sandals for this is holy ground." Moses hid his face because he was afraid to look at God. God told Moses that it was his job to bring the Israelites out of Egypt. At first, Moses protested. What an overwhelming mission! But God told Moses that he would help Moses free his people from slavery.

Teacher Notes:

Young children understand that fire is hot and can burn them. This is a good opportunity to talk about fire safety and the danger of playing with lighters or matches. This craft technique uses a source of heat – a warming tray – and melted crayons. Remind children that the tray is hot. Use caution: work with one child at a time.

Older children will want to know why the fire did not consume the burning bush. Was it a magic trick or an optical illusion? Explain that this is a miracle story and that the voice gave Moses a vision of God's plan for the Hebrews. Again, remind children to be careful around the melting wax.

Burning Bush Collage

Objectives:
- Children will follow directions to create a collage of twigs and melted wax.
- Older children will learn the term "collage" and enjoy a new art technique under supervision.
- Children will remember Moses' mission to set his people free.

Materials: warming tray or cookie tray, aluminum foil, paper towels, wax crayon bits and pieces in warm colors (red, orange, yellow, pink and magenta), 9 in. x 12 in. yellow or pastel construction paper, glue, bits of twigs, either green tissue paper or Q-tips, and green tempera paint for painting leaves

Preparation: Cover the surface of the tray or cookie sheet with aluminum foil. Plug in the warming tray in a safe area where it cannot be knocked or pulled over. Allow to heat on lowest setting.

Procedure:

1. Have children recall what God said to Moses from the burning bush. Ask, "How do you think Moses felt when he heard God's voice? What colors could we use to show the bush on fire?"

2. Remind children that the tray is hot. Use caution. Work with one child at a time to melt crayons. Have each child choose a color of construction paper. Allow one child to rub several colors of wax crayon in concentric circles on the aluminum foil as shown (or have younger children watch as you do this step).

3. Demonstrate how to place the construction paper face down on the melted wax and press to create a wax print. Help each child to make his wax print, wiping the foil with a paper towel after each application.

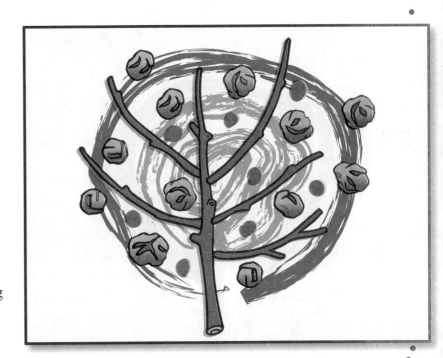

4. Have children glue twigs to the wax print.

5. Children can either glue tissue paper leaves to the wax print or use Q-tips to paint green leaves on the wax print.

6. Label the collage of the burning bush with these words: "God Speaks to Moses."

Moses Gets Pharaoh's Attention

Exodus 7:2–13

Moses and his brother Aaron went to plead with Pharaoh to free the Hebrew slaves. Neither was sure that Pharaoh would listen to them, but they followed God's instructions. Moses said to Pharaoh, "The Lord God of the Hebrews says, 'Let my people go.'"

God had already told them what to do if Pharaoh demanded to see a miracle in order to believe that God sent them. God said, "Take thy rod and cast it before Pharaoh and it shall become a serpent." So Aaron threw down his rod, and it became a snake. Pharaoh's magicians did the same, but Aaron's snake swallowed up their snakes. This made Pharaoh angry, and he refused to set the Hebrews free.

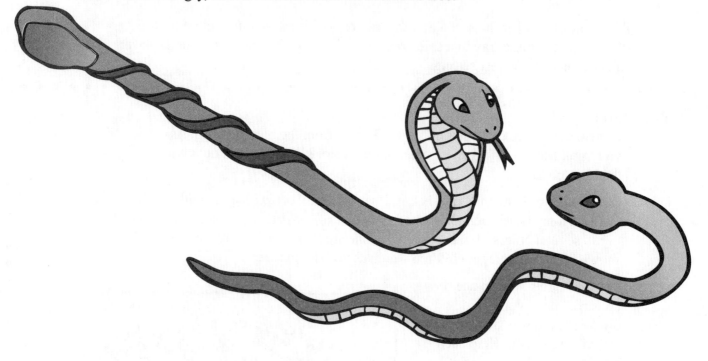

Teacher Notes:
Young children can re-enact the scene and remember the words, "Let my people go." Preschoolers can touch and describe a sample of snakeskin. They can describe how snakes move and pretend to slither on their bellies like snakes.

Older children can discuss what they would do to get Pharaoh's attention. Children can retell the story and listen to a recorded version of "Let My People Go." They can discuss why some people have a fear of snakes and identify some poisonous as well as helpful snakes.

Rods Turned Into Serpents

Objectives:
- Children use fine motor skills to create and texturize play-dough snakes.
- Older children can paint and decorate their snakes.

Materials: teacher-made play-dough (page 95); plastic forks and knives; rollers and kitchen tools for printing such as a mallet, grater, or slotted spoon; photos of real snakes; sample of snakeskin; tempera paints and brushes if desired; newspaper

Preparation: Prepare sufficient hardening play-dough from the cooked cornstarch recipe on page 95. Do **not** add food coloring.

Procedure:
1. Ask children to recall what God told Moses to say to Pharaoh. Ask, "How did Moses get Pharaoh's attention? What happened when Aaron's staff turned into a snake?"

2. Display photos of real snakes and a sample of snakeskin if available. Have children feel the snakeskin or describe the snakes' appearance.

3. Provide each child with a small amount of dough to roll into a snake shape. Help young children manipulate the long snakes to create curves, a head, and a tail. Texturize the snakeskin with rollers, mallets, toothpicks or other clay tools.

4. Allow the snakes to harden through time if children will be painting them.

5. Have children paint their snakes with a base coat of tempera paint and then use a sponge to rub with a contrasting color to bring out the texture of the snakeskin.

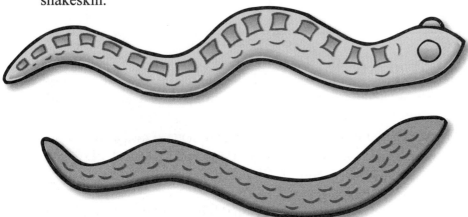

A Plague of Frogs

Exodus 8:1-15, Exodus 9-10

Pharaoh's heart was hard. He refused to let the Hebrews go. So God sent a plague of frogs to cover Egypt. The frogs hopped up from the Nile River. They were everywhere – in Pharaoh's palace, in his bed, on his table. Pharaoh called for Moses. "Pray to your God to make the frogs go away. Then I'll let the people go," said Pharaoh. So Moses prayed and God took the frogs away. But stubborn Pharaoh changed his mind, and the Hebrews remained as slaves. Then God sent plagues of flies, disease, hail, locusts, and three days of darkness, among other disasters!

Teacher Notes:
Young children can understand that Pharaoh was *stubborn*. Discuss when they can be stubborn or unwilling to listen to parents. They can pretend to be frogs hopping on Pharaoh's bed. Have them imagine what a room full of frogs would sound like!

Older children can compare the ten plagues of Egypt to natural disasters such as drought and floods, volcanic eruptions, tsunamis, and tornadoes. They can look up frog facts online to share with one another.

Frog Prints and Jumping Frogs

Objectives:
- Children will learn the word *plague.*
- Young children can sponge paint frogs.
- Older children can cut and paste to create pop-up jumping frogs.
- Children will remember the story of a stubborn Pharaoh and a persistent Moses.

Materials: frog pattern on page 83, tag board, sponges, green and brown tempera paint in shallow dishes, yellow and green construction paper, newspaper, pencils, glue, pairs of wiggle eyes or precut black construction paper circles, one 1 in. x 5 in. strip of construction paper per child

Preparation: Duplicate the frog pattern on page 83. Trace onto tag board several times and cut out to create frog stencils. Save the cutout frogs for children to trace onto green construction paper to make pop-up frogs later. Cover the tables with newspaper. Provide wet sponges and tempera paint in shallow dishes.

Procedure:
1. Have children imagine what the plague of frogs must have looked like. Have them make sounds like a room full of frogs. "Ribbit!"

2. Give each child a piece of 9 in. x 11 in. construction paper and a frog stencil.

3. Demonstrate how to sponge paint overlapping frogs.

4. Allow each child to choose a color of paint and to sponge paint a plague of frogs.

5. To make jumping frogs, have each child trace and cut out a frog from green construction paper. Glue on wiggle eyes or black paper circles for eyes as shown. Accordion fold the 1 in. x 5 in. strip of paper and glue on the underside of each frog. Attach the other end of the folded strip to a 9 in. x 12 in. piece of construction paper.

Exodus 8:6   Exodus 8:6   Exodus 8:6   Exodus 8:6

Chased by Chariots

Exodus 14:5-30

Although Pharaoh said he would let the Israelites go, he changed his mind. After all, who would do all of the work if the slaves were set free? As Moses and his people were fleeing from Egypt, Pharaoh set out with 600 chariots in pursuit.

The Israelites had camped for the night on the banks of the Red Sea. When the people saw Pharaoh's army approaching, they feared for their lives. They prayed to the Lord. God told Moses what to do. Moses lifted up his rod and the waters divided and the sea became dry land. The Israelites escaped, but the chariots chasing them were not so lucky. Moses raised his rod again, and the waters returned – drowning the entire army. That day the Lord saved Israel. The people believed God, and they followed Moses into the wilderness.

Teacher Notes:
Young children can learn new vocabulary, including the words *chariot, Israelites,* and *Red Sea.* They can act out being chased by chariots in a game of Red Rover.

Older children can locate the Red Sea on a map and identify the countries in the area including Egypt, Israel, and Saudi Arabia. Have them compare modern military transportation to Pharaoh's army of chariots. Compare chariot racing in ancient times to NASCAR races today.

Discuss the practice of slavery in ancient times with older children and discuss why Moses, Abraham Lincoln, Martin Luther King, Jr., and Nelson Mandela are considered heroes by many people all over the world.

"Let My People Go!" Bumper Stickers

Objectives:
- Young children can trace and color to create bumper stickers for the Israelites.
- Older children can create logos for chariot teams.
- Children will remember the story of a stubborn Pharaoh, a persistent Moses, and how God created a miracle to save his people.

Materials: colored copy paper, crayons or markers, samples of bumper stickers or team logos, scissors or paper cutter

Preparation: Cut enough colored paper into bumper sticker sizes on a paper cutter.

Procedure:
1. Ask children where they have seen bumper stickers or decals. Ask them to describe some messages they remember.
2. Ask, "What kinds of messages might the Israelites have had on their vehicles?"
3. Provide each child with a bumper sticker pattern and crayons.
4. Discuss the words, "Let My People Go!" and ask children, "Who said these words? What do they mean?"
5. Have young children trace the words and add their own illustrations.
6. Older children can work in pairs to come up with a chariot team name and draw their logos.

Moses Comes Down From Mount Sinai

Exodus 19-21, 32-34

God told Moses to climb to the top of Mt. Sinai. There, God gave Moses the Ten Commandments. The list of God's rules was carved into two stone tablets. The Ten Commandments are God's important rules that tell us how to live.

After forty days, Moses came down from the mountain to share the Ten Commandments with his people. However, while waiting for Moses, the people had made a huge golden calf to worship. They were dancing and bowing down to the statue. Moses was very angry that, while he was gone, the people had already broken one of God's sacred commandments. He threw down the stone tablets, and they broke into pieces. He went back up the mountain for another forty days and prayed to God to forgive the people for their sins. God gave Moses a second set of tablets.

I. I AM THE LORD YOUR GOD. DO NOT PUT ANY OTHER GODS BEFORE ME.
II. DO NOT TAKE THE LORD'S NAME IN VAIN.
III. KEEP HOLY THE SABBATH.
IV. HONOR YOUR FATHER AND MOTHER.
V. YOU SHALL NOT KILL.
VI. YOU SHALL NOT COMMIT ADULTERY.
VII. YOU SHALL NOT STEAL.
VIII. YOU SHALL NOT LIE (BEAR FALSE WITNESS).
IX. YOU SHALL NOT COVET YOUR NEIGHBOR'S WIFE.
X. YOU SHALL NOT COVET YOUR NEIGHBOR'S GOODS.

Teacher Notes:
Young children will not understand all of the commandments. By age five, however, they are able to understand that we need rules to live in our families, in our classrooms, and in our communities. Discuss what rules they need to be happy and safe in your classroom. Share God's rules for living.

Older children will be interested in learning about early forms of writing such as carvings in stone, writing on papyrus or parchment, Egyptian hieroglyphics, and printing on clay tablets. They can compare ways of early forms of writing throughout history to modern printing and word processing techniques and learn to write Roman numerals.

The Ten Commandments Cookie

Objectives:
- Children can learn and print Roman numerals in play-dough or clay.
- Children can count to ten and create a big cookie to bake, break, and share.
- Children will remember the story of Moses and the Ten Commandments carved into stone.

Materials: one package of refrigerated sugar cookie dough, pizza pan, oven, oven mitt or potholders, plastic gloves, craft sticks, clay or play-dough, napkins, paper towels and sponges for cleanup

Preparation: Sanitize tables or counter for food preparation. Refrigerate prepared sugar cookie dough until class time. Preheat the oven according to the directions on the package.

Procedure:

1. Ask children to recall what was carved on the two stone tablets in the story. Ask, "Why did Moses throw down the tablets?"

2. Provide clay or play-dough and craft sticks for children to practice writing Roman numerals.

3. Then tell them they will be making a big Ten Commandments cookie to share.

4. Have children wash hands and don plastic gloves to help spread the cookie dough onto the pizza pan. Shape the dough into two tablets.

5. Help children to use craft sticks to "carve" Roman numerals into the dough.

6. Bake the dough as directed on the package until golden brown.

7. Cool the big cookie. Pass out napkins and have children break off pieces to eat as they retell the story of the Ten Commandments and recall what God's laws are in order.

The Walls Come Tumbling Down

Joshua 6:1-20

After Moses died, Joshua became the leader of the Hebrews. Joshua and the army of Israel were about to attack the city of Jericho, but the walls surrounding the city were heavily fortified. God gave Joshua an unusual plan. He said, "March around the city wall each day for six days. Carry the Holy Ark of the Covenant. Do not make a sound except for the sound of the trumpets of the priests."

This did not sound like a battle plan, but the soldiers did what Joshua told them to do. Each day they made a huge parade marching around the city wall. On the seventh day, they marched around the wall seven times in silence. Then the trumpets sounded and the soldiers gave out a roar. Miraculously, the walls of Jericho tumbled down! Joshua and his army took the city because they had listened to the Lord.

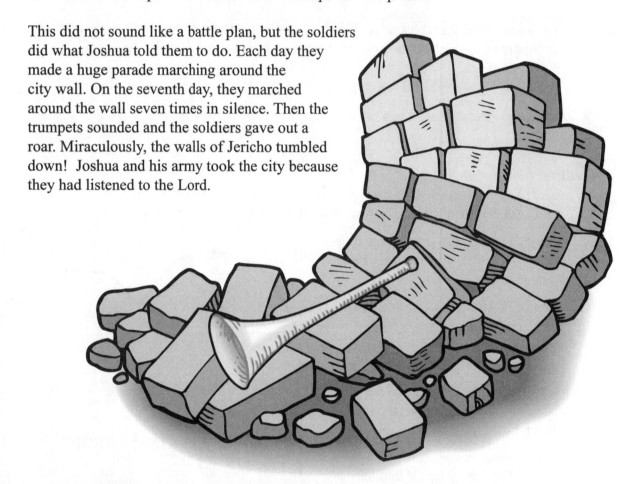

Teacher Notes:
Young children will enjoy marching and making a loud noise with their trumpets on cue.

Older children can explore the idea of walled cities and brainstorm strategies for taking the city. Discuss why God's plan was an unusual strategy.

Jericho Noise Makers

Objectives:
- Children will use listening and fine motor skills to make trumpet noisemakers.
- Young children will count to seven as they march around outside on the playground and use their imaginations to "blow the walls down."
- Older children will learn about walled cities and discuss military strategies to take the city of Jericho.

Materials: one paper towel tube per child, tissue paper, scissors, glue, rubber bands

Preparation: Cut two 6 in. x 9 in. tissue paper strips per child and one 5 in. x 5 in. tissue paper square for each child.

Procedure:
1. Ask children to recall the story of Jericho. Ask, "What did God tell Joshua and his army to do? Why was this plan better than storming the walls?" Have older children brainstorm other strategies to get inside the city. Tell children they will be making a lot of noise outside with their own trumpet noisemakers.

2. Give each child a paper towel tube and demonstrate how to wrap and glue it with a 6 in. x 9 in. tissue paper strip.

3. Demonstrate how to cover one end of the tube with the 5 in. x 5 in. tissue square and attach with a rubber band.

4. Demonstrate how to wrap and glue the second 6 in. x 9 in. tissue paper strip around the tube as shown and make cuts to create a fringe.

5. Demonstrate how to blow into the tube to make a noise.

6. Take the noisemakers outside for a parade and "blow the walls down" on cue!

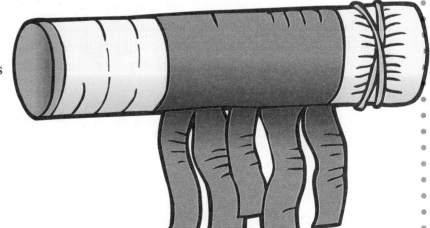

David Stands Up to a Giant Goliath

I Samuel 17:19–52

Saul and the army of Israelites were preparing to fight the Philistine army. The battle lines had been drawn. The army camps were set up on two opposite hills. Each morning for forty days, a huge Philistine soldier named Goliath would appear in front of the camps and dare Saul's soldiers to send someone to fight him. No one dared go.

David was just a young shepherd boy but, when he heard Goliath's dare, he decided he could fight the nine-foot giant and win with God's help. He told Saul that God had saved him from a lion and a bear. He was not afraid of Goliath because God would help him again. With plenty of stones in the fields and plenty of practice herding sheep, young David had become an excellent marksman!

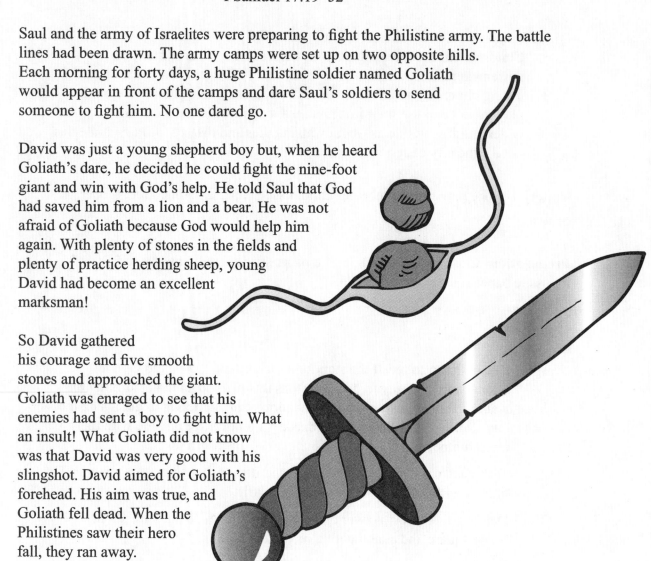

So David gathered his courage and five smooth stones and approached the giant. Goliath was enraged to see that his enemies had sent a boy to fight him. What an insult! What Goliath did not know was that David was very good with his slingshot. David aimed for Goliath's forehead. His aim was true, and Goliath fell dead. When the Philistines saw their hero fall, they ran away.

Teacher Notes:
David learned at an early age to use a slingshot to herd his sheep. He used the tools of his trade to defeat his enemy. However, children should know that slingshots could kill.

- Discuss with young children the dangers of throwing stones or other projectiles.

- Older children can compare Goliath to other giants in familiar fairy tales or folktales such as "Jack in the Beanstalk" and "Paul Bunyan." Children can measure their heights and compare to giants in literature.

Prayer Pebbles

Objectives:
- Children will follow directions and use fine motor skills to decorate prayer pebbles to remind them that God is with them.
- Children will discuss the dangers of throwing rocks.

Materials: clean, small river stones available at garden stores, tubes of acrylic paint in various colors, newspaper, measuring tape, can of shellac, and wide brushes

Preparation: Collect river stones and wash clean if needed. Cover the tables with newspaper.

Procedure:
1. Ask, "What is a giant? What stories do you remember that have giants in them?" Ask children to recall the story of David and Goliath. Ask, "How tall was this giant? Why did David think he could fight Goliath?" Measure the height of several children and compare to the nine-foot Goliath.

2. Ask, "What is a slingshot? What would happen if you fired a slingshot at somebody?" Have children discuss the dangers of throwing stones. Tell them they will be making prayer pebbles to carry in their pockets.

3. Provide each child with a smooth stone and allow him to choose a color of paint.

4. Children paint their rocks to create a prayer pebble. Older children can paint a chapter and verse numbers on their stones, if desired. When paints dry, the teacher brushes the stones with clear shellac.

5. Tell children to carry the prayer stones in their pockets to remind them that God is with them.

David Becomes King

I Samuel 18:6-15; 20:12-17; 24:1-22, 31:1-7; 2 Samuel 5:1-5

After killing Goliath, David was made a general in Saul's army. David won so many battles that he became a super hero to the Israelites. The fact that David was so popular made King Saul jealous and suspicious. He sent David on the most dangerous missions. But God was with David, and he came back victorious and even more popular.

When David married Saul's daughter, Saul was even more afraid that David would try to take over his kingdom. Saul's thinking became so twisted that he ordered his son Jonathan to kill David. But Jonathan and David were best friends forever. Jonathan warned David to run and hide.

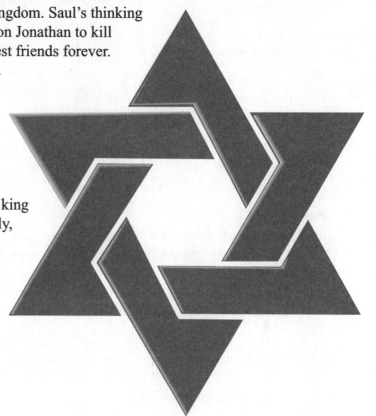

King Saul's soldiers hunted David day and night. One night David had the chance to kill Saul who was asleep in a cave. But David refused to kill the king. Instead he cut a piece from Saul's robe to show that he would not hurt the king even when he had the chance. Eventually, Saul and his sons were killed in battle by the Philistines, and the people made David king. David was a great king. He ruled Judah and Israel for forty years and made Jerusalem the center of his kingdom. His sign is the Star of David.

Teacher Notes:
Help young children create a Star of David. Discuss what it means to be best friends like Jonathan and David.

Older children may have favorite super heroes or comic book heroes and can compare their heroes to David. They enjoy comic books and can use their imaginations and creative writing skills to create their own action adventure story about David. They can identify feelings of friendship, jealousy, and mistrust, and they can create dialogue in speech bubbles.

Super Hero's Star of David

Objectives:
- Children will follow directions and use fine motor skills to create a Star of David.
- Older children can share favorite super hero stories and create their own action adventure comic strip about David.

Materials: masking tape, pre-cut sentence strips (4 in. x 36 in.), craft sticks, glue, glitter, yarn, scissors, newsprint, colored markers, several super hero comic books

Preparation: Collect several comic books that feature super heroes such as Superman, Spiderman, and Batman. Write each sentence below on an individual sentence strip for children to sequence.

Procedure:

1. Ask, "Who is your favorite superhero or action figure?" Allow children to share some adventure stories featuring their heroes. Tell children they will illustrate the story of a Bible super hero.

2. Share the story of David and have children sequence the following sentence strips:
   - David kills Goliath.
   - David becomes a popular general.
   - King Saul sends David on a dangerous mission.
   - David marries King Saul's daughter.
   - King Saul orders his son Jonathan to kill David.
   - Jonathan tells David to run and hide.
   - David finds Saul sleeping in a cave, but does not kill him.
   - David finds out that Philistines have killed Saul and his sons.
   - The people make David their king.

3. Assign children partners, and give each pair a sentence strip and piece of newsprint. Provide colored markers. Have them illustrate their sentence strip on the newsprint.

4. Tape the pictures in sequence to the wall to create a storyboard.

5. To make the Star of David, have children glue craft sticks, as shown, into a star shape. Children may add glitter with glue. Then cut and tie a piece of yarn to hang.

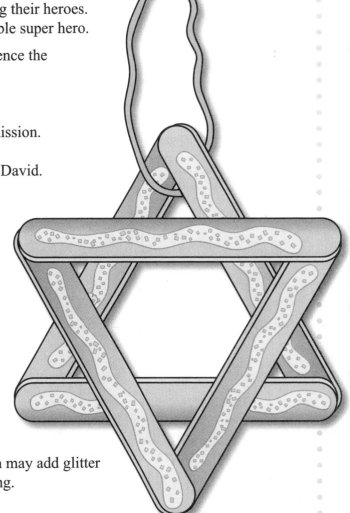

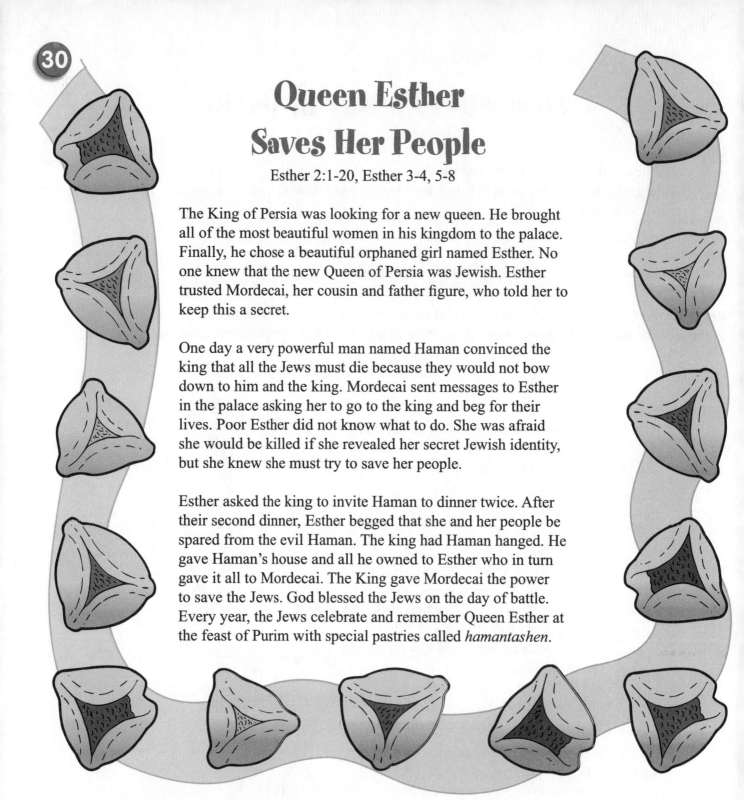

Queen Esther
Saves Her People

Esther 2:1-20, Esther 3-4, 5-8

The King of Persia was looking for a new queen. He brought all of the most beautiful women in his kingdom to the palace. Finally, he chose a beautiful orphaned girl named Esther. No one knew that the new Queen of Persia was Jewish. Esther trusted Mordecai, her cousin and father figure, who told her to keep this a secret.

One day a very powerful man named Haman convinced the king that all the Jews must die because they would not bow down to him and the king. Mordecai sent messages to Esther in the palace asking her to go to the king and beg for their lives. Poor Esther did not know what to do. She was afraid she would be killed if she revealed her secret Jewish identity, but she knew she must try to save her people.

Esther asked the king to invite Haman to dinner twice. After their second dinner, Esther begged that she and her people be spared from the evil Haman. The king had Haman hanged. He gave Haman's house and all he owned to Esther who in turn gave it all to Mordecai. The King gave Mordecai the power to save the Jews. God blessed the Jews on the day of battle. Every year, the Jews celebrate and remember Queen Esther at the feast of Purim with special pastries called *hamantashen*.

Teacher Notes:
Girls may dress up like Queen Esther and hold a beauty pageant of Esthers. Provide old sheets and pillow cases and ribbons to create royal gowns. Boys can dress up like the King of Persia. Have children decorate paper crowns with glitter glue and markers for the event.

Older children will enjoy making *hamantashen* pastries to share.

Hamantashen Pastries

Objectives:
- Children will follow a simple recipe to make traditional pastries served at Purim.
- Children will remember how Queen Esther risked her life to save her people.

Materials: strawberry or raspberry jam and prepared dough (see recipe below), cookie sheet, 3-inch cookie cutter, rolling pin, waxed paper, oven mitt or pot holder, teaspoon, plastic gloves, paper towels, napkins, large chart paper, marker, recipe

Hamantashen Pastries

Ingredients:
- 2/3 c. margarine
- ½ c. sugar
- ¼ c. orange juice
- 1 c. wheat flour and 1 c. white flour
- strawberry and/or raspberry jam

Directions:
Blend margarine and sugar in a bowl.
Add flour and orange juice, alternating to make soft dough.
Refrigerate for several hours.
Roll thin dough between sheets of waxed paper.
Cut out 3-in. circles.
Spoon a teaspoon of jam in the center of each circle.
Fold edges of dough in to make a triangle shape.
Bake at 375 degrees for 10-15 minutes. (Makes 24.)

Preparation: Write the recipe on a large piece of chart paper. Prepare dough the day before and keep refrigerated until activity. Sanitize tables for food preparation.

Procedure:

1. Ask children to recall the story of Queen Esther. Ask, "Why was Esther scared? Who was the evil man who ordered that all Jews be killed?"

2. Introduce the word *hamantashen.* Tell children they will be making these triangle-shaped Haman's hats. Together read the recipe steps.

3. Preheat the oven and don the plastic gloves and place ¼ of the dough between two sheets of waxed paper. Flatten and roll out the dough as thin as possible.

4. Allow each child to use the cookie cutter to cut out a 3-in. circle.

5. Have each child place a teaspoon of jam in the center of his circle.

6. Demonstrate how to fold and overlap the dough, as shown, to form a triangle.

7. Place the "hats" on the cookie sheet.

8. Bake as directed. Cool and serve hamantashen as children recall the story of Esther.

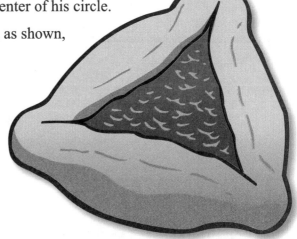

32

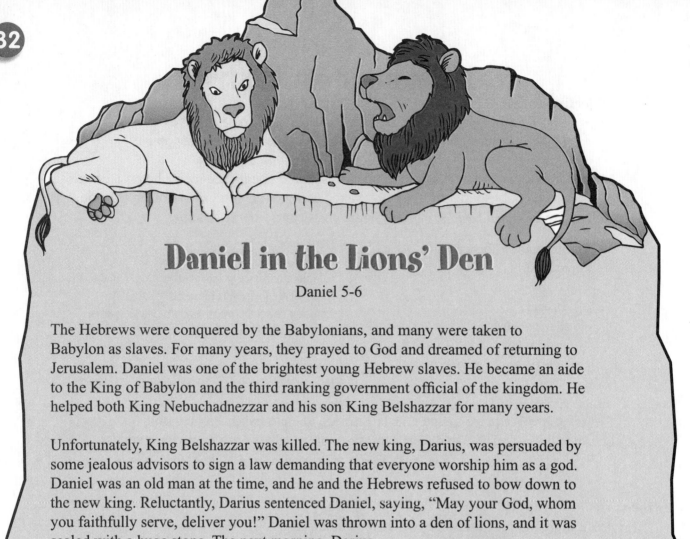

Daniel in the Lions' Den

Daniel 5-6

The Hebrews were conquered by the Babylonians, and many were taken to Babylon as slaves. For many years, they prayed to God and dreamed of returning to Jerusalem. Daniel was one of the brightest young Hebrew slaves. He became an aide to the King of Babylon and the third ranking government official of the kingdom. He helped both King Nebuchadnezzar and his son King Belshazzar for many years.

Unfortunately, King Belshazzar was killed. The new king, Darius, was persuaded by some jealous advisors to sign a law demanding that everyone worship him as a god. Daniel was an old man at the time, and he and the Hebrews refused to bow down to the new king. Reluctantly, Darius sentenced Daniel, saying, "May your God, whom you faithfully serve, deliver you!" Daniel was thrown into a den of lions, and it was sealed with a huge stone. The next morning, Darius watched as the stone was rolled away. Daniel was still alive! God had sent an angel to keep the lions' mouths shut. The king and the Babylonians were convinced of the power of Daniel's God.

Teacher Notes:
Young children may have seen lions at the zoo or circus. Discuss where lions live and what they eat. Introduce children to a group of lions in a photo and tell children that the family is called a *pride* and their home is called a *den*. Have them identify the male, female, and cubs, and compare lions to other big cats.

Older children can locate Babylon and Jerusalem on a map. They can recall that this is yet another time in the history of the Jews when they were in slavery. Introduce the words *exile* and *refugee*. Have children identify how they might feel if they were forced to leave their homes and live in exile.

A Lion Mask

Objectives:

- Children will use listening and fine motor skills to make lion masks.
- Young children will learn new vocabulary including *pride, den*, and *cubs*.
- Young children will use their imaginations to use the lion masks to roar like lions.
- Children will understand that because Daniel was faithful to God, he was saved from death in the lions' den.

Materials: photo of a pride of lions, one 10-in. paper plate per child, black and yellow construction paper, circle templates and ear patterns on page 85, scissors, glue, 6-in. lengths of brown yarn, black markers

Preparation: Reproduce the patterns on page 85 on tag board to create templates. Cut out six lengths of brown yarn for each child.

Procedure:

1. Ask children to recall the story of "Daniel in the Lions' Den." Ask, "Why was Daniel thrown in with the lions? What happened to him?"

2. Show the photo of lions and have children identify the male, female, and cubs. Have children tell what they know about lions. Tell children they will make lion masks.

3. Have each child trace and cut out six yellow circles (3 ½ in. in diameter), one black circle (3 ½ in. in diameter), and two black circles (1 in. in diameter.) Children also trace and cut out two yellow ears.

4. Children arrange four yellow circles on their paper plates and glue as shown.

5. They position and glue one large black circle in the center of each plate.

6. Next, glue the ears, as shown.

7. Help position and glue the two remaining yellow circles atop the brown circle, as shown. Children add dots and whiskers with black marker.

8. Bundle several lengths of yarn and wrap and tie in the center of each bundle. Children glue the yarn as shown to create the lion's mane.

9. Young children will enjoy holding the masks in front of their faces and roaring like lions.

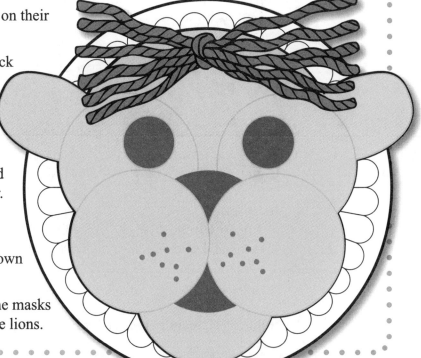

Jonah in the Belly of the Whale

Jonah 1-3

Jonah was called by God to go to the evil city of Nineveh to preach. But Jonah did not listen to God. Instead he ran away. He went down to the docks of Joppa and boarded a ship on its way to Tarshish taking him far away from Nineveh.

During the night while Jonah was sleeping below deck, God created a terrible storm at sea. Huge waves pounded the ship and the howling wind blew the sails to pieces. The sailors were so afraid that they woke Jonah and begged him to pray to his God to save them all. Jonah knew that God was punishing him. In order to stop the storm, he told the crew to throw him overboard. The sailors felt they had no choice. So into the raging sea went Jonah!

Lucky for Jonah he wasn't swallowed by a shark! Instead, God sent a huge fish, probably a whale, to swallow Jonah whole. For the next three days and nights, Jonah lay in the belly of the whale. He asked God to forgive him. Then God caused the whale to spit Jonah out. Jonah was washed ashore. When he came to, he was on dry land and very thankful.

God had given him a second chance to do his work. Jonah went to Nineveh and warned them to change their evil ways or God would destroy the city. The people listened, and God forgave them. Both the people of Nineveh and Jonah were saved.

Teacher Notes:
Children can act out the story of "Jonah in the Belly of the Whale." Create a storm at sea with sound effects and fans blowing wind. After the crew throws Jonah overboard, have the children throw a blanket over him to represent being swallowed by the whale.

Older children can identify types of whales and learn facts about whales.

A Whale of a Tale

Objectives:
- Children will follow directions and use fine motor skills to create a whale that swallows Jonah and gold fish crackers.
- Older children can learn facts about blue whales.

Materials: whale template and Jonah pattern on page 84, one 9 in. x 12 in. piece of blue construction paper per child, one 3 in. x 5 in. piece of white paper per child, one round coffee filter per child, scissors, pencils, black marker, glue, craft sticks, plastic gloves, gold fish crackers, crayons

Preparation: Duplicate the whale and Jonah pattern on page 84 and create several templates of each.

Procedure:
1. Provide each child with a piece of blue construction paper. Have the child fold his paper in half, then place the whale template so that the bottom of the whale is on the fold and trace around it with pencil.

2. Each child cuts out the whale and adds an eye, fin and blowhole with black marker.

3. Have each child fold his coffee filter into a pie shape and cut slits as shown to create a waterspout.

4. Children apply glue along the inside edge of each whale and glue their folded coffee filters inside, as shown. Cut a slit for the mouth and leave the mouth of the whale open.

5. Each child traces Jonah on white paper, colors it, cuts it out, and glues it to a craft stick. The child can insert the stick puppet in his whale's mouth.

6. Place gold fish crackers in additional coffee filters to eat. Children can pull Jonah in and out as they retell the story and eat gold fish crackers.

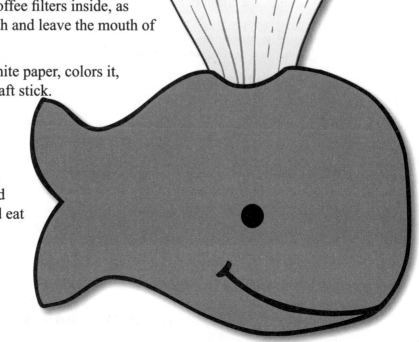

An Angel Speaks to Mary

Luke 1:26-38

Mary was a young girl living in the small town of Nazareth in Galilee. She was engaged to Joseph. One day an angel appeared to Mary and told her that she was to become the mother of the Messiah. The Jews had been waiting for a messiah, or savior, for hundreds of years.

"Do not be afraid," said the angel Gabriel. "You have found favor with God. You will have a son, and you will name him Jesus."

"How can this be?" Mary wondered.

"All things are possible with God," said the angel.

Remember that, throughout history and in the Bible, angels were sent as messengers from God. In this case, Gabriel had a VERY important message for the world about Jesus. Mary and Joseph would be parents to Jesus, and we would have a Savior!

Teacher Notes:
Young children will have lots of questions about angels. Start the discussion by displaying images of angels or looking for them in church. Together, make a chart listing what children know and what they want to know about angels.

Older children can find names of angels in the Bible, including Michael and Gabriel and recall the role that angels played in bringing messages to Mary, Joseph, and the shepherds at Christmas. Then sing along to the Christmas carols "Angels We Have Heard on High" and "Hark the Herald Angels Sing."

Coffee Filter Angel

Objectives:
- Older children can identify angels as symbols of Christmas and understand that God uses angels as his messengers.
- Children will create and name angels for a bulletin board display.

Materials: one coffee filter per child, white tempera paint, plastic spoon, 9 in. x 12 in. colored construction paper, cotton balls, glue, glitter, scissors, yellow or black curling ribbon OR bits of pink or yellow Easter grass, newspaper, stapler, paint brush

Preparation: Cover tables with newspaper. Cover bulletin board with blue paper.

Procedure:

1. Ask children what they know about angels. Ask, "What did the angel Gabriel tell Mary?" "How would you feel if an angel came into our classroom? What would you do?"

2. Provide each child with a piece of construction paper. Have children fold their papers in half lengthwise.

3. Demonstrate how to spoon a quarter-size amount of paint between the folds and press outward as shown to make angel wings. Sprinkle wings with glitter. Paint a small circle in the middle of the paper toward the bottom of the wings for a head and allow to dry.

4. Have children cut their coffee filters in half and cut two slits as shown. Cut the remaining half in half again. Position the coffee filter shapes on the paper as shown and use dots of glue to assemble the angel's robe.

5. Glue cotton balls beneath the angel's robe to create a cloud.

6. Use scissors to cut and curl ribbon, then glue to create hair **OR** arrange and glue pink or yellow Easter grass for hair.

7. Have children name their angels and recall the message Gabriel gave to Mary.

8. Display the student-created angels on a bulletin board entitled, "A Host of Heavenly Angels."

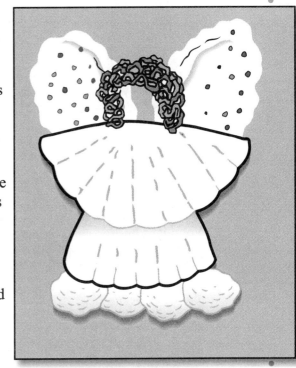

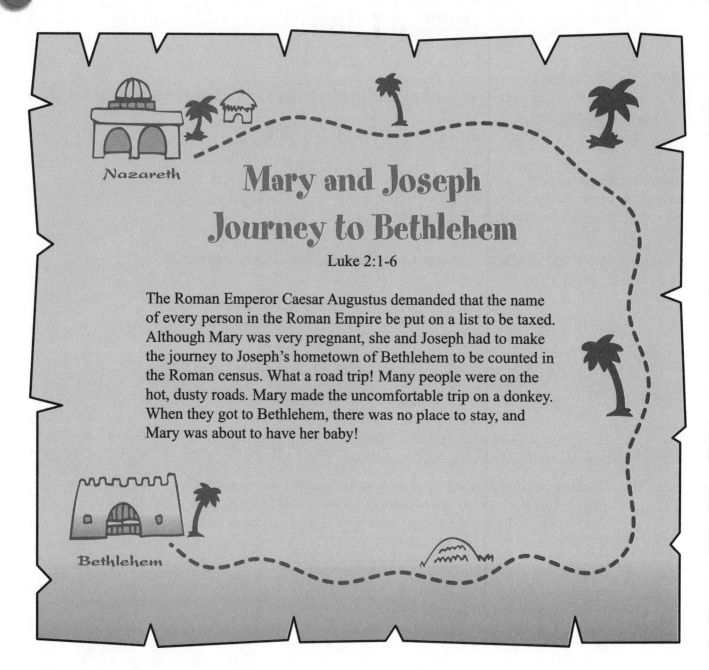

Mary and Joseph Journey to Bethlehem

Luke 2:1-6

The Roman Emperor Caesar Augustus demanded that the name of every person in the Roman Empire be put on a list to be taxed. Although Mary was very pregnant, she and Joseph had to make the journey to Joseph's hometown of Bethlehem to be counted in the Roman census. What a road trip! Many people were on the hot, dusty roads. Mary made the uncomfortable trip on a donkey. When they got to Bethlehem, there was no place to stay, and Mary was about to have her baby!

Nazareth

Bethlehem

Teacher Notes:
Younger children can compare riding on a donkey to road trips they have taken. If possible, visit a petting zoo so children can see animals of the nativity.

Older children can compare beasts of burden such as donkeys, camels, horses, mules, elephants, and llamas. Have older children locate Nazareth, Bethlehem, and the Jordan River on a map of the Middle East and discuss means of transportation in Jesus' time.

Donkey Christmas Ornaments

Objectives:

- Older children can compare beasts of burden. Young children can identify and describe a donkey and compare it to a horse.
- Children can follow directions to make donkey Christmas ornaments.

Materials: photo of a donkey, non-clip clothespin per child, tempera paints, brushes, newspaper, sponges, crayons, yarn, glue, scissors, small wiggle eyes, Christmas card showing Mary riding a donkey on the way to Bethlehem

Preparation: Reproduce the patterns on page 86 on white paper. Cut ribbon into 9-inch lengths.

Procedure:

1. Show children the photo of the donkey and have them identify the animal. Ask, "Why is the donkey an important part of the Christmas story?" Show the Christmas card. Ask, "Why were Mary and Joseph on the road to Bethlehem? How do you think Mary felt about the trip?"

2. Tell children they can create a donkey Christmas tree ornament.

3. Provide non-clip clothespin and one set of patterns per child.

4. Have each child color and cut out the donkey patterns and decorate as shown. Glue the donkey head to a clothespin and glue on wiggle eyes.

5. Hang the clothespin on a Christmas tree.

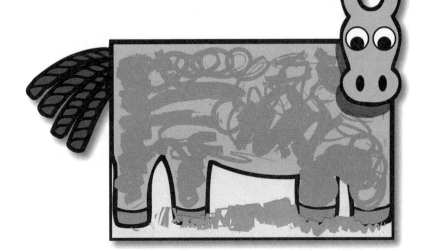

No Room at the Inn

Luke 2:7

When they got to Bethlehem, Mary and Joseph were very tired, but there were no rooms available at the inn. So they found shelter in a cave with the farm animals. That night Jesus was born. Mary wrapped him in cloth and placed him in the manger. The cows, sheep, chickens, and the donkey were the first ones to see the Baby Jesus.

Teacher Notes:
Young children can identify the nativity animals and the sounds they make. They can learn the words *manger, straw,* and *inn* and use fine motor skills to create a bed for the Baby Jesus.

Older children can share their experiences traveling with their families and perhaps staying at motels. They can imagine the smells and sounds of the manger scene if they have been to a barnyard.

Baby in a Manger

Objectives:
- Young children can learn the words *nativity* and *manger.*
- Children can follow directions to make a baby in a manger.
- Children can color, cut, and fold the stand-up characters to create a nativity scene.

Materials: one coffee filter and one craft stick or balsa wood spoon per child, straw or craft raffia, glue, scissors, white tissue paper, crayons, animal patterns on page 88, white construction paper, black marker, cardboard

Preparation: Reproduce the patterns on page 88 on white paper for children to color and cut out.

Procedure:
1. Ask, "Which animals do you think saw the Baby Jesus first?" Ask, "What sounds did Baby Jesus hear?" Have children describe the sights, sounds, and smells in the nativity.

2. Provide each child with the patterns. Have children color and cut out the patterns. Glue each animal or character to a folded piece of cardboard to stand up.

3. Have each child cut pieces of raffia and glue in the center of his coffee filter to represent straw.

4. Have each child wrap his wooden spoon in a strip of white tissue paper and draw eyes with the marker.

5. Place the baby Jesus in the center of the straw. Children can stand up the animals around the manger to create a nativity scene.

Shepherds Hear the News

Luke 2:8-20

Who came to see the Baby Jesus? Shepherds watching their flocks that night were told the Good news by an angel of the Lord. The angel said, "Do not be afraid; for see, I am bringing you Good News of great joy to all people. To you is born this day in the city of David a Savior who is the Messiah, the Lord...You will find the baby wrapped in bands of cloth and lying in a manger." Then suddenly the angel was joined by a host of angels singing and praising God. When the angels disappeared, the shepherds decided to go to Bethlehem and see for themselves.

Teacher Notes:
Five-and six-year-olds know all about babies, or so they think. They will want to talk about their new siblings and all the preparations that are necessary before a baby arrives. They can learn the new vocabulary words: *announcement, Messiah,* and *a host of heavenly angels.*

Older children can identify with the shepherds who were frightened but curious about the birth announcement. Ask older children how we would share the joyful news of a Savior today. Would it be on CNN? Online? On the radio? In the newspapers? Older children may read birth announcements in the local newspaper. Help them to create announcements to send to friends or family to announce Jesus' birth.

It's a Boy! Birth Announcements

Objectives:
- Children will share their family preparations for the arrival of new babies.
- Children will use fine motor skills to cut and paste pictures of babies to make birth announcements.
- Children will understand that Jesus came into the world as a baby boy and grew up to be our Savior.

Materials: a birth announcement, crayons, photos of babies in magazines, white glue or glue sticks, one 9 in. x 12 in. piece of baby blue or white paper per child, black marker to label cards, a diaper bag with baby items such as disposable diapers, baby wipes, bib, bottle, and toys

Preparation: Gather magazines with photos of babies of all races. Place the magazines and construction paper on the art table, and provide scissors, glue sticks, and a black marker at each table.

Procedure:
1. Ask, "What is fun about having a new brother or sister? What is not fun? What things do we need to have for a new baby? Where do babies sleep? Where did Baby Jesus sleep?"

2. Then open the diaper bag and ask, "What things might be in this diaper bag to take care of Baby Jesus?" Allow children to name some items; then have one child at a time reach in the bag, pull out an item, and tell how Mary might use it to care for Baby Jesus.

3. When all items have been discussed, ask, "How do you think Mary and Joseph felt when they had a baby boy?" Allow children to come up with answers that may range from happy and worried to proud and tired. Then explain that, when they were born, their parents were so proud they might have sent announcements to tell friends and family. Show the example of the birth announcement and read the words. Tell children, "Your parents may have even sent a picture of you with the announcement."

4. Tell children they will be making announcements of Jesus' birth to give to friends or family. Ask, "What could the card say?" "What is the date? What will be the time? Who are the proud parents?"

5. Demonstrate how to fold and label the card and paste a photo of a baby inside. Provide each child with crayons and help him fold the paper and label it to make a card. Allow each child to choose a baby picture to paste inside his card and to add details of the nativity with crayons. Use the black marker to label each card with the date and time. Children write "It's a Boy!" with crayons.

Wise Men from the East

Matthew 2:1-12

When Jesus was born in Bethlehem in the days of King Herod, three wise men came to Jerusalem. These wise men had heard about a prophecy and followed a star from the east in search of a new king. They asked, "Where is the child who has been born King of the Jews? We have come to pay him homage."

King Herod was worried by the news of a new king. He consulted his priests, and they told him that it had been foretold that the ruler of Israel would be born in Judea. So Herod told the wise men to go to Bethlehem and to report back to him once they found the young child.

Teacher Notes:
Young children can act out the three wise men following the star. Provide props such as paper crowns, robes, and presents. They can brainstorm what presents they would bring to a baby king. Young children will count three wise men, three camels, and three gifts.

Older children will be interested in the gifts of *frankincense* and *myrrh,* which were precious oils and perfumes uses to preserve mummies of kings. Compare them to the smell of incense and scented candles. Older children can compare gold, *frankincense,* and *myrrh* to modern day precious gifts.

Follow the Star

Objectives:
- Children will recall the story of the three wise men and the Star of Bethlehem.
- They can learn the meaning of *prophecy, frankincense* and *myrrh.*
- Children will use several techniques to create a starry sky above Bethlehem.

Materials: one 3 in. x 12 in. strip of brown construction paper, one 9 in. x 12 in. piece of black construction paper per child, camel patterns on page 87, colored markers, glue, star templates, pencils, silver glitter, scissors, Christmas cards depicting the three wise men, paint brushes, white tempera paint, shallow pan of water, sponge, newspaper

Preparation: Reproduce the patterns on page 87 on white paper for children to color. Cut the brown paper into strips. Cover tables with newspaper.

Procedure:

1. Show children the Christmas cards and have them retell the story. Ask, "Why were the wise men following the star?" Share that Jesus' birth had been foretold by a *prophecy.* Explain that a prophet is someone who listens to God and tells the future. The people of Israel had been waiting for their King for many years.

2. Ask, "Where did the star lead the three wise men?" Tell children they will be making a picture showing the starry sky above Bethlehem.

3. Give each child a piece of black construction paper. Demonstrate how to wet the paper with a sponge and water. Use a paintbrush to drop spots of white tempera paint onto the wet paper. Watch as the stars appear.

4. While papers are drying, have students color and cut out the camel patterns.

5. To create the Star of Bethlehem, trace or draw a large star in the starry sky, as shown. Then outline this star with glue. Next, sprinkle with silver glitter. Shake off any excess glitter over the newspaper.

6. Have each child glue the strip of brown paper to the bottom of his black construction paper. Glue the three camels facing the Eastern Star.

Jesus as a Child in the Temple

Luke 2:42 – 51

When Jesus was twelve, his parents took him to Jerusalem for the feast of the Passover. When they left the city and started back home, they thought Jesus was with their group. However, at the end of the day, they discovered that their son was missing! After three days, they found Jesus in the Temple. Jesus was sitting with the priests and teachers asking questions and answering their questions.

Mary and Joseph were very upset with Jesus, but they were also very relieved to see him. The young Jesus was surprised that they were so worried. He explained that he had been fine the whole time. He had stayed in his Father's house. He was not afraid because he had been with God in the Temple. Jesus went home to Nazareth with his parents and was obedient to them.

Teacher Notes:

Young children can understand why their parents would be frantic if they got lost in a store or busy mall. Take this opportunity to remind children about personal safety. Children can recall rules about strangers: always stay with parents or a group for safety, and never go with strangers. They should be taught to seek help from a police officer or uniformed security guard.

Older students can understand how Jesus' curiosity got him in trouble. Perhaps they, too, have been so absorbed or interested in something that they forgot the time, missed deadlines, and failed to complete tasks. Discuss the natural consequences of such actions. Ask, "Who is hurt when we cause others to worry or when we are unreliable?"

Stained Glass Windows

Objectives:
- Children will recall the story of a young Jesus in the Temple.
- Children will compare the Temple to their church.
- Children will be reminded that the church is our Father's House.
- Children will learn a stained glass technique using melted wax.

Materials: one 9 in. x 12 in. piece of black construction paper per child, glue, scissors, crayons, waxed paper, iron, newspapers, hole punch, one 9 in. length of yarn per child

Preparation: Cover table with layers of newspaper. Preheat iron on low.

Procedure:

1. Have children recall the story and discuss when they may have become separated from their parents or their friends. Ask, "Have you ever gotten lost? How did you feel?" Have children share their experiences and tell what happened when they were found. Ask, "Did Jesus mean to worry his parents? Where was he for three days, and why was he not afraid? Why did he call the temple 'My Father's House?'"

2. Have children compare the Temple of Jerusalem to their own church. Older children can learn that the Holy Temple was a very special place in Jerusalem. It was where Jews came to worship, where the priests studied, and where God was glorified. It took King Solomon seven years to build the first Temple.

3. Tell children, "Some houses of God have windows with beautiful, colored glass called *stained glass*." If possible, take children on a tour of the church or show pictures of stained glass windows. Tell children they can create the stained glass effect with melted crayons.

4. Provide each child with a piece of black construction paper. Have each child fold it in half and draw and cut out a frame, leaving the fold intact.

5. Give each child a piece of waxed paper to fold in half. Demonstrate how to use scissors to make crayon shavings.

6. Children shave crayons inside their folded waxed paper. Carefully, have each child place his folded waxed paper atop the layers of newspaper. Press with the iron on low heat just till the shavings melt.

7. Have each child insert his "stained glass" in the folded frame, trim to fit, and glue around the edges.

8. Punch a hole in the top of the frame, run the yarn through it and tie the yarn to make a hanger.

9. Display the stained glass windows by hanging them in the classroom windows.

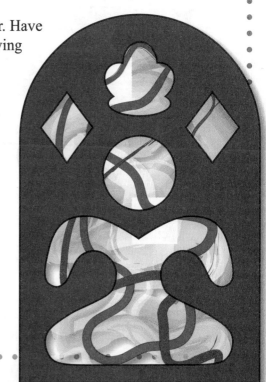

Jesus Is Baptized

Matthew 3:1-17

What a scene it was at the Jordan River! People came from all across Judea, walking for miles in the desert, and lining up on the riverbank to see John the Baptist. He looked a little strange dressed in clothing made of camels' hair with a leather belt around his waist. The word was that he ate locusts and wild honey, but he also had a reputation for being a powerful preacher. He baptised people by dipping them in the water. He washed them clean of their sins and told them to get ready for the Messiah.

John was also a cousin of Jesus. One day, Jesus came to John to be baptized. Jesus went into the river. John realized that Jesus was sent from God. John put Jesus under the water. Just as Jesus emerged soaking wet, the sky split open and the Holy Spirit came down to Jesus looking like a dove above his head. Then God spoke from heaven in a voice that shook the earth: "This is my Son, the Beloved, with whom I am well pleased."

Everyone who saw the dove come down from heaven and heard the voice of God that day knew that Jesus had the Holy Spirit in him.

Teacher Notes:
Young children are intrigued by our church ritual of baptism. They want to know how and why. They can understand that baptism is a sacrament that welcomes them into God's family. Be prepared for plenty of questions about the Holy Spirit as they assimilate this new information.

Children age six to ten like to perform, and this re-enactment will give them a visual reminder of what happened at Jesus' baptism. Older children can act out this dramatic scene from the Bible, adding special sound effects.

The Holy Spirit Door Hanger

Objectives:
- Children will recall the events of Jesus' baptism and act out the scene.
- Children will identify the dove as the symbol of the Holy Spirit.
- Children will recall their own baptism and make a dove door hanger as a reminder that God's spirit is always with them.

Materials: examples of the Holy Spirit depicted as a dove, one dove pattern (page 93) per child, one 4 in. x 9 in. strip of colored tag board per child, scissors, crayons or markers, 3-in. circle template, pencil, laminating film if desired

Preparation: Reproduce the dove pattern on page 93 on white paper for each child. Precut the tag board into strips, one per child.

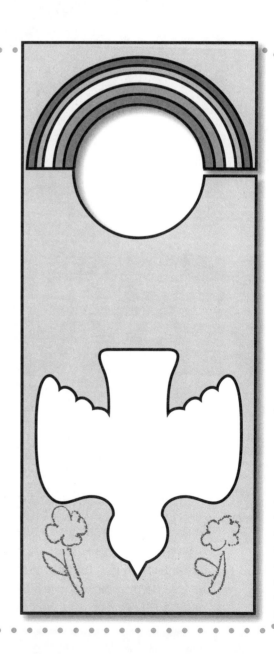

Procedure:
1. Discuss the atmosphere on the banks of the Jordan River. Ask, "Do you think the scene was crowded? Hot? Dusty? Quiet? Exciting? What would you have seen, heard, smelled, and touched as an onlooker in the crowd? How did John baptize people? What happened that was unusual when Jesus was baptized? What would you think as you walked away?"

2. Ask, "How were you baptized?" Explain the full emersion method and compare to the baptism of infants at the baptismal font. Explain that the Holy Spirit comes to us at baptism.

3. Show examples of how the dove is used as a representation of the Holy Spirit or take children go to the narthex and sanctuary if possible to look for symbols of the Holy Spirit.

4. Provide each child with a strip of colored tag board and a dove pattern to cut out.

5. Have each child trace a 3-in. circle with pencil on his tag board strip and cut out as shown. The child glues the dove to his door hanger and writes a message, "The Holy Spirit Is In!" Children may use crayons or markers to decorate their door hangers. Laminate for durability if desired.

Fishing on the Sea of Galilee

Luke 5:1-11

Simon Peter and his brother Andrew were fishermen by trade. They dropped their nets on the Sea of Galilee. Sometimes their nets would be full, but one night they fished all night with no luck. The next day, Peter saw Jesus approaching his boat with a large crowd of people following him. Jesus asked Peter if he could hop aboard Peter's fishing boat. They pulled away from the shore a little, and Jesus preached to the crowd from just off shore.

Then Jesus said, "Go out into the deep water and drop your nets." Peter and Andrew did this, and the nets were so full of fish that they could hardly pull them in. The boat was beginning to sink! What a catch!

Jesus said, "From now on you will be catching people." Peter and Andrew decided right there to follow Jesus. They left their boat and nets and became Jesus' first disciples.

Teacher Notes:
Young children can re-enact fishing from Peter's boat, casting nets and bringing in many fish. They can learn the meaning of the word *disciple*. Older children can understand the commitment it takes to leave family and jobs to do God's work.

School-age children can compare different fishing methods and learn about different kinds of fish that are caught in nets. Remind children that some people are concerned that tuna fishermen often catch other sea creatures such as sea turtles and porpoises. Lead students in a discussion comparing modern day fishing methods to God's call to be good stewards of the earth.

What a Catch!

Objectives:
- Children will recall how Simon Peter and Andrew fished on the Sea of Galilee and became fishers of men.
- Young children can glue fish cutouts or die-cut foam fish and netting and plastic wrap to create Sea of Galilee pictures.
- Young children will use fine motor skills to tie goldfish crackers in netting.

Materials: foam fish, glue, 9 in. x 12 in. piece of heavy weight blue construction paper or tag board per child, net bags from produce, ribbon, scissors, colored markers, tape, plastic wrap, goldfish crackers

Preparation: Precut netting into squares. Place ¼-cup goldfish crackers in a paper cup for each child.

Procedure:
1. Share the story and ask children, "How do you think Simon Peter and Andrew felt when Jesus asked them to drop the nets where they assumed no fish could be caught? How did they feel when they pulled in nets that were full?"

2. Ask, "What did Jesus mean when he said that they would fish for men? Would many people quit their jobs to follow Jesus today?"

3. Have children write "What a Catch!" with markers and glue their foam fish randomly on their construction paper.

4. Demonstrate how to wrap each picture in plastic wrap, and secure on the back with tape.

5. Show children how to secure netting with tape over their fish.

6. Give each child a ¼ cup of goldfish crackers. Provide each child with a square of netting and demonstrate how to gather the goldfish crackers and tie the ribbon.

7. Allow children to sample some goldfish as they work, and have each child take his catch-of-the-day home.

Feeding the Crowd

Matthew 14:13-21; Luke 9:10-17

Huge crowds wanted to hear Jesus preach. People followed Jesus and his disciples even as they tried to find a place to rest and relax. One day about five thousand people gathered on a hillside listening to Jesus. It was late in the day, and the people were hungry and tired. The disciples were tired too. They came to Jesus and said, "The people are hungry, and they have no food. Tell them to go home!"

To their surprise and dismay, Jesus told his disciples to find food for all the people–an overwhelming, impossible task. The disciples went into the crowd and found only five loaves and two fishes. Then Jesus told everyone to sit down on the grass. As the crowd watched, he blessed the food and broke it into pieces. He gave it to his disciples to pass out to the crowd. He told them to collect any leftovers. After feeding the thousands, there were twelve baskets of food left over! Jesus knew God would provide enough for everyone. He had wanted to teach his disciples to trust him and to trust God.

Teacher Notes:
Children can break bread into pieces to share. They can pass the bread in a basket as they re-enact the scene. They can compare kinds of bread all over the world. Explain that Jesus probably used flat bread or unleavened bread rather than the white bread we use for sandwiches. Unleavened bread has no yeast or sugar added.

Older children can compare the scene to their own experiences with crowds, perhaps waiting in lines to buy food at sporting events or music concerts. They can identify with the disciples feeling overwhelmed with the task of feeding five thousand people. Discuss how they can problem-solve together to accomplish a task that seems impossible.

Fishes and Loaves Lunch Bag

Objectives:
- Children will learn about *unleavened bread* and compare to other types of bread.
- Children will recall how Jesus fed five thousand people and taught his disciples to trust God.
- Children will decorate a lunch bag with fishes and loaves.

Materials: one brown paper lunch bag per child, fish and loaf templates, (pages 89-90) brown markers, bread basket, five loaves of whole wheat pita or Middle Eastern flat bread, scissors, brown and white construction paper, pencils, fish stamps and stamp pad if desired

Preparation: Place the five loaves of bread in the basket. Reproduce the patterns on page 89 and 90 for each child. Trace onto tag board to make several sets of templates.

Procedure:
1. Share the story and ask children, "How do you think the disciples felt when Jesus told them to find food for the five thousand people? How much food did the disciples collect? What did Jesus do with the five loaves and two fishes?"

2. Show the basket with the five loaves inside. Have children compare this flat bread to the white sandwich bread common in American culture. Explain that, in Jesus' time and in many countries today, bread is not made with yeast. The bread dough does not rise when it is baked. This is called *unleavened* bread.

3. Pass the basket and have each child break off a piece of pita or flat bread to eat.

4. Provide a brown paper bag and brown and white construction paper for each child.

5. Have children stamp or trace fish on the paper bag. Then have them each trace and cut out two brown fish and five white loaves from construction paper.

6. The children place their cut out loaves and fishes in the bag to take home.

How Big Is a Mustard Seed?

Matthew 13:31-32

Jesus told many stories or parables so that the people could understand and remember his lessons. One story was about having faith the size of a mustard seed. Mustard seeds are tiny seeds, but they send out roots and grow into large, strong trees in the garden. Jesus told his disciples that the kingdom of God starts like the little mustard seed that sends out roots and grows into a great faith.

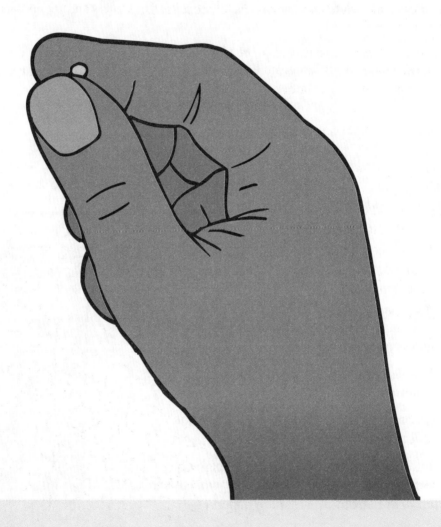

Teacher Notes:
Have children examine and compare different kinds of seeds. Remember that tiny mustard seeds are difficult for small children to pick up and glue. Dried navy beans and lima beans are easier for them to manipulate. Older children can collect and label seeds from fruits. Young children can discover how seeds germinate by placing lima bean seeds in a zippered plastic bag with wet paper towels and watching the roots sprout. Place sealed bags in a sunny window. Keep seeds moist and watch through a few days.

Bean and Seed Collage

Objectives:
- Children will compare the size of a mustard seed to other seeds and dried beans.
- Children will recall how Jesus fed five thousand people and taught his disciples to trust God.
- Children will create a collage with seeds and dried beans.

Materials: one container or jar of mustard seed; bags of dried lentils, popcorn kernels, navy beans, and lima beans; glue; heavy weight construction paper or poster board; pencils

Preparation: Place the different kinds of dried beans and seeds in individual egg carton sections, shallow containers, or baskets.

Procedure:
1. Show the children the mustard seeds. Compare to the top of a straight pin. Share the story and ask children, "What did Jesus mean when he said the kingdom of heaven is like a mustard seed? What can a little bit of faith do?"

2. Show the other kinds of seeds and beans and have children try to identify each kind. Children can compare the seeds and beans and guess what kind of plant it came from.

3. Tell them they can choose from any of the beans and seeds to make a *collage.*

4. Provide each child with a piece of heavy construction paper or poster board.

5. Have children glue beans and seeds to create their own original designs.

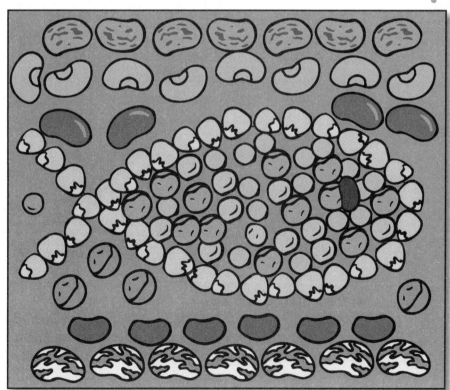

Who Is the Good Samaritan?

Luke 10:25-37

One day an expert on Jewish law asked Jesus, "What do I need to do to get into heaven?"

Jesus asked in return, "What does God's law say?"

The man replied, "It says to love the Lord your God with all you heart, and with all your soul, and with all your strength, and with all your mind and to love your neighbor as much as yourself. But who is my neighbor?"

Then Jesus told the *parable* of a Samaritan who stopped to help an injured man. The man had been robbed and beaten and left to die along the roadside. In Jesus' story, a priest passed by and did not help even though the injured man was a Jew. A second man, a leader in the church, saw the injured man but kept on walking.

The helpless man was near death when the Samaritan heard his groans. Although the Jews and Samaritans had been enemies for hundreds of years, the Good Samaritan came to his aid. He washed his enemy's wounds with wine and applied olive oil so the wounds would heal. Then the Samaritan helped the Jewish man onto his donkey and took him into town. The Samaritan gave the innkeeper money to care for the injured man until he was strong again.

"Who was a true neighbor to the man who was robbed?" asked Jesus. All who heard this story knew that Jesus wants us to care for everybody in need, not just friends and family. We are called to love everyone.

Teacher Notes:
The story of the Good Samaritan will bring up questions such as, "When is it safe to come to the aid of a stranger? What can children do to help?" Remind children that they can go to a parent, police officer, or a safe place if they need help or if they see a stranger in trouble. Children as young as four can understand that a stranger should never ask a child to go with him to help find a pet or to show the way. Older children can locate information about the Red Cross online at www.redcross.org to discover ways to help people in need.

Make a First Aid Kit

Objectives:
- Children will recall how the Good Samaritan helped the man in need.
- Children will create first aid kits for the car or home.

Materials: one plastic storage box with lid container per child, checklist of first aid items including band aids, antibacterial cream, individually wrapped gauze bandages, surgical tape, wet wipes, latex gloves, cotton swabs, and scissors, one index card per child, pencils, red construction paper, clear tape or laminating film, sample classroom first aid kit, picture of the Red Cross emblem, contact information for local emergency services and Poison Control

Preparation: Ask parents to donate supplies for first aid kits. Send home a request and collect and sort supplies through time.

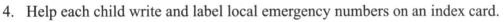

Procedure:
1. Discuss what being a Good Samaritan means. Ask, "What did the Samaritan do to help the injured man? Who comes to our rescue now in emergencies?" Discuss the role of Emergency Medical Teams and the training that they must have in First Aid and CPR.

2. Show the children the picture of the Red Cross emblem. Ask children if they know what the symbol stands for and explain the mission of the organization to provide aid to communities during natural disasters and to relieve suffering.

3. Give each child a piece of red construction paper. Have each child draw and cut out a red cross and tape it to his box lid.

4. Help each child write and label local emergency numbers on an index card.

5. Children assemble their kits using the checklist.

Build Your House Upon a Rock

Matthew 7:24-29, Luke 6:46-49

Jesus preached that, if you hear and follow the word of God and have a strong foundation of faith, you will be like the man who built his house upon the rock. When the rains fell and the floods came, his house was not washed away. The one who hears and does not follow is like the foolish man who builds his house on sand that will be swept away when the flood comes.

Jesus told this story to end his Sermon on the Mount. He wanted the people to change their lives. He wants us to build a strong foundation of faith so that, when hard times come, we will be strong.

Teacher Notes:
Young children will remember this story better if they can actually build a sandcastle and wash it away in a sandbox.

School-age children love collections and may have rock collections to share. If possible, have each child bring in a rock. Compare rocks and try to identify the hardness on the hardness scale.

Older children will enjoy learning about home building from a local builder or contractor. They can study blueprints or house plans, and learn some terms and building materials. They will remember the importance of pouring a strong foundation.

Dream House Diorama

Objectives:
- Each child will design his dream room and create a three-dimensional diorama.
- Children will recall the lesson of building on a strong foundation.

Materials: examples of house plans or blueprints, craft sticks, glue, shoeboxes, fabric and construction paper scraps, wall paper samples, and paint chips

Preparation: Have each child bring in a shoebox. Obtain paint chips and wall paper samples from a home improvement store.

Procedure:
1. Discuss what Jesus meant when he said, "Build your house upon the rock."

2. In preparation for building an "Extreme Makeover Dream House" with shoebox rooms, give each child a piece of white construction paper. Have him design a room in his dream house.

3. Provide markers, glue, paper, and fabric scraps. Each child decorates the inside of his shoebox to create a dream room diorama.

4. Stack the boxes for a "Build Your Dream House" display if desired.

Saving the Lost Sheep

Luke 15

The parable of the lost sheep reminds us that we are all important in the eyes of God.

Jesus asked the religious leaders or Pharisees, "If you had one hundred sheep and lost one, wouldn't you leave the ninety-nine and look for the one who was lost? Wouldn't you be joyful when your sheep is found and tell your friends and neighbors?" Jesus said, "It will be the same in heaven. The angels will rejoice more when one sinner turns from sin than for all the righteous others who need no repentance."

Jesus told this story to show the Pharisees that God loves even the sinners who have said they are sorry and want to follow God.

Teacher Notes:
Young children will be able to act out the shepherd and the one lost sheep. They can express how it feels to find a favorite toy or security blanket that had been lost. They can learn the words *rejoice* and *joyful*.

Peer pressure gets more intense with age. Belonging to the right group and being "cool" are very important even by age seven. Schoolagers will understand that the Pharisees were upset with Jesus for hanging out with the wrong people. He ate meals with tax collectors, prostitutes, and sinners. Jesus treated everyone just the same. He showed them that God loved and valued each person no matter what their sins when they turned to him. Children this age can discuss how not being with the "in" group makes them feel and what they can do to show that they accept and respect all classmates.

Lost Sheep Stick Puppets

Objectives:
- Children will remember that they are all loveable and capable in God's eyes.
- Each child will create a sheep stick puppet and a shepherd stick puppet.

Materials: sheep and shepherd patterns on page 91, craft sticks, glue, white construction paper, cotton balls, scissors, crayons or colored markers, shoebox

Preparation: Reproduce the patterns on white construction paper for each child to color and cut out. Cut slits in the shoebox as shown.

Procedure:
1. Discuss the story and ask, "Why did Jesus say there would be much rejoicing when just one sinner turns from sin?"

2. Tell children they will each make a sheep stick puppet. Have each child color and cut out the patterns and glue them to his craft sticks.

3. Children can glue cotton balls on their sheep.

4. Have the children stand up their sheep in the shoebox to represent the flock.

The Tax Collector Climbs a Tree

Luke 19

Zacchaeus was a chief tax collector who lived in Jericho. He collected taxes for the Romans. He pocketed a lot of the money himself, so he was very rich. No one liked or trusted Zacchaeus, especially not the Jews. He was also a very short man.

One day Jesus came to Jericho. Huge crowds of people wanted to see him. They followed him through the streets and pushed and shoved to get close to him. Zacchaeus wanted to see Jesus too. In fact, he was so determined to see who Jesus was that he climbed a sycamore tree! Then Zacchaeus waited for Jesus and the crowd to come by. When Jesus looked up, he saw Zacchaeus hanging on to the tree branch. "Come down, Zacchaeus," said Jesus. "I want to have dinner at your house tonight."

The people were angry. Why was Jesus visiting the home of this man they all hated? But Jesus knew that Zacchaeus needed to hear about God's love for him. That day, Jesus changed Zacchaeus forever. Zacchaeus said he was sorry for cheating people, and he gave half of all his possessions to the poor.

Teacher Notes:
Young children will be able to identify with being short and wanting to get a better view in a crowd. Have them brainstorm other ways they use to secure a better view–standing on tiptoes, ladders, and sitting on Daddy's shoulders come to mind. Bring in a step ladder to act out the story if you wish.

Older children can donate to a charity or food bank for the poor.

Zacchaeus in the Sycamore Tree

Objectives:
- Children will remember the story of Zacchaeus and how his life changed after meeting Jesus.
- Each child will create a pop-up of Zacchaeus climbing the sycamore tree.

Materials: white construction paper, green tissue paper, scissors, crayons or colored markers, 9-in. lengths of yarn, pattern below, paper clip per child

Preparation: Reproduce the patterns on white construction paper for each child to color and cut out.

Procedure:

1. Discuss the story and ask, "Why was Zacchaeus hated? Why did Zacchaeus want to see Jesus? Why were the people upset with Jesus? Would you have climbed a tree to see Jesus?" Tell children they will help Zacchaeus climb a tree.

2. Provide the patterns for children to color and cut out.

3. Cut two slits in the tree as shown.

4. Thread a piece of yarn through both slits and tie on the back of the tree.

5. Paper clip Zacchaeus to the yarn so when pulled, he climbs to the top.

6. Have children roll up small bits of tissue paper into little balls and glue to their trees for leaves if desired.

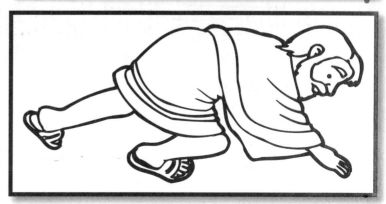

Pattern

Jesus Enters Jerusalem

Matthew 21:1-11, Mark 11:1-10, Luke 19:28-40

The time had come for Jesus to enter the holy city of Jerusalem. But he did not want to march in like a powerful king. He told his disciples to find him a donkey to ride. The people heard he was coming and lined the streets. As he rode into the city, some people cut palm leaves or leafy branches and laid them down before Jesus to honor him. It was obvious that many people believed that Jesus was the King of the Jews. This troubled the chief priests, the scribes, and the elders.

Teacher Notes:
Young children can re-enact the scene of Jesus entering Jerusalem. Provide palms on Palm Sunday and have children carry them as they march around the church. Older children can prepare for Easter by planning an Easter egg hunt for younger children or by visiting a nursing home or retirement community to color Easter eggs.

Palm Sunday Welcome Banner

Objectives:
- Children will create a banner to welcome Jesus.
- Each child will remember how Jesus entered Jerusalem in triumph.

Materials: white bulletin board paper, markers, sponges, green tempera paint, palm fronds, newspaper, shallow pans of water, sample of a "Welcome Home" banner

Preparation: Gather examples of banners or pennants ahead of time. Cover the tables with newspaper.

Procedure:

1. Have children compare the arrival of Jesus in Jerusalem to the arrival of a famous person in their town or city. Ask, "How would you welcome a famous sports team, returning soldiers, or a movie or rock star to your town? What would you do if you were on the welcoming committee?"

2. Show the sample banners or pennants. Tell children they will make a welcome banner for Jesus. Provide paper, markers, green tempera paint, sponges, and water.

3. Demonstrate how to lay the palm leaves down on the bulletin board paper and sponge paint to create an outline.

4. Have children sponge paint over the palm leaves to create a banner welcoming Jesus and springtime. Allow to dry and display the banner in the classroom or hallways.

The Last Supper

Matthew 26:17-35; Mark 14:10-32

Jesus and the twelve disciples celebrated the Passover meal in an upstairs room in Jerusalem. Jesus knew he was going to die soon. This would be the last supper they would all have together. As a teacher, Jesus wanted to leave his disciples with a reminder of all they had learned. He took the bread and blessed it and broke it and said, "This is my body." He gave the bread to the disciples to eat. Then Jesus picked up the cup of wine and said, "This is my blood. Do this to remember me." The disciples drank from the cup of wine.

Jesus said to his disciples, "One of your will betray me." Peter said, "Not one of us would do such a thing." But he was wrong. One disciple named Judas had already betrayed Jesus. He had made a deal with the priests to turn Jesus over to his enemies.

Teacher Notes:
Children will see the connection between the Last Supper and the Sunday Eucharist. Older children can learn the names of the twelve disciples and re-enact the scene of the Last Supper.

The Cup of Wine Mosaic

Objectives:
- Children will learn the word *mosaic* and use fine motor skills to create a paper chalice using a mosaic technique.
- Children learn that the outward appearance of the bread and wine do not change during the consecration when they become the body and blood of Jesus.

Materials: colored tissue paper squares, one plastic wine glass per child, glue or wallpaper paste, wide brushes, newspaper, church chalice, wine, unblessed hosts or bread, altar cloths, example or picture of a mosaic picture created with ceramic tiles or stones

Preparation: Cover the tables with newspaper. Precut tissue paper into 1-inch squares. Place the elements of the Eucharist on a tray and cover with altar cloths to show how they are prepared and placed on the altar.

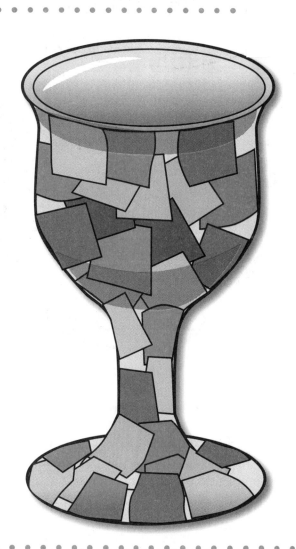

Procedure:
1. Have children recall the story of the Last Supper. Show them the elements of the Eucharist and have them identify the items as you unveil the cup and bread. Ask, "What does the bread remind us of? What does the wine remind us of?"

2. Tell children that they will be decorating a wine chalice as a reminder that Jesus' holy blood was shed for us and for our sins. Show them the example or picture of a mosaic technique created with tile or stone.

3. Provide each child with a plastic wine glass, tissue paper squares, white glue and brushes.

4. Demonstrate how to cover the glass with glue and overlap the tissue paper to make a mosaic effect.

5. Allow each child to choose colors and decorate his wine glass. Allow glue to dry.

Peter Hears the Rooster Crow

Mark 14:66-68; Luke 22:31-34; Matthew 26:33-35

...ook Peter, James, and John with him to the Garden of Gethsemane, a quiet park ...he could pray. Jesus said to his disciples, "Tonight you will all run away, but I ...e you later in Galilee." Peter protested, "Lord, I will never leave you." But Jesus ...to Peter and said, "You, Peter, will deny me three times before the cock crows ...n the morning."

...esus prayed while they slept. In the night, Judas came with some soldiers. ...rested Jesus and tied him up. The disciples ran away, and Jesus was taken as a ...r before the Roman governor, Pilate.

...as very scared but he wanted to find out where they had taken Jesus. What had ...of his best friend and teacher? Peter managed to get close to some soldiers so ...l hear what they were saying about his friend Jesus. Just then a servant pointed ...t and said, "You were with Jesus!" Peter said, "No, you're wrong. I don't know

...ied knowing Jesus twice more. The third time, as Peter was speaking, a rooster crowed again. This all happened just as Jesus had predicted. Peter wept.

Teacher Notes:
Younger children will learn that roosters crow at sunrise, and they can pretend to crow like roosters greeting the morning.

Older children will understand that Jesus' predictions came true. Judas betrayed him, and Peter denied knowing him. Older children can understand how the disciples felt when their friend and teacher was taken away. They can make a list of emotions including ashamed, scared, helpless, and confused. What would they have done to save Jesus?

A Rooster at Sunrise

Objectives:
- Children will create a sunrise scene with watercolor paints and learn the word *silhouette*.
- Children will remember that a rooster crowed to greet the morning that Jesus died.

Materials: watercolors and paint brushes or colored washable markers, coffee filters, shallow pan of water, scissors, 5-in. black construction paper squares one per child, glue, picture of a real rooster, rooster pattern on page 92, pencils

Preparation: Reproduce the rooster pattern on page 92 and cut out several rooster templates. Precut black construction paper squares. Cover the tables with newspaper.

Procedure:
1. Have children recall the story and how Peter denied that Jesus was his friend three times. Ask, "How do you think Peter felt when the soldiers took Jesus? How do you think Peter felt when the rooster crowed? Have you ever felt ashamed of something you said or did?" Remind children that Jesus loved Peter anyway and that God still loves them when they make mistakes or do something that makes them feel ashamed or guilty.

2. Show children a picture of a real rooster. Explain to young children that the rooster crows to greet the morning at sunrise. Tell children they will be creating a sunrise with watercolors and rooster *silhouettes*.

3. Provide each child with a coffee filter and demonstrate how to apply paint or colored washable markers in wide strokes to create a sunrise. Use yellow for the center.

4. Have each child dip his colored filter in the pan of water till just wet and watch the colors blend around the yellow sun. Allow filters to dry.

5. Provide each child with a black construction paper square. Children trace roosters with pencil and cut them out. Children then glue their roosters in the center of the filters.

6. Have children take their sunrises home to share the story of Peter.

Jesus is Crucified

Matthew 27:24-54; Mark 15:16-39; Luke 23:13-47; John 19:17-28

Jesus was given a death sentence. He was to be put to death on a cross. The soldiers placed a crown of thorns on his head and made fun of him. They forced him to carry his heavy cross through the streets to a hill. They nailed his hands and feet to the cross and raised it on the hill between two criminals also nailed to crosses.

At the foot of the cross, Jesus' mother, John, and Mary Magdalene watched helplessly. Jesus looked down from the cross and saw them standing together. Jesus told his mother. "John is your son now." He said to John, "This woman is your mother now."

Jesus suffered terribly but he forgave his enemies from the cross. When Jesus died, the sky was dark, the earth shook, and there was a loud noise. Many people thought it was the end of the world. Today we call this day Good Friday.

Teacher Notes:
Younger children can explore the thorns on a long stemmed rose and learn about plants that have thorns.

Older children can make a list comparing Jesus, King of the Jews, to royalty. Jesus wore a crown of thorns rather than a gold crown. He served others rather than demanding others serve him. He was poor rather than rich.

Older children can discuss and understand why Jesus wanted John to take care of his mother.

A Crown of Thorns

Objectives:
- Children will create a crown of thorns to remember the Crucifixion.
- Children will learn the word *royalty* and remember that Jesus is our King.

Materials: one white paper plate per child, elbow macaroni, glue, scissors, pictures of royalty wearing crowns, real long stemmed rose or cactus with thorns

Preparation: Cover the tables with newspaper. Provide elbow macaroni in bowls at each table.

Procedure:

1. Have children recall the story and how the soldiers made fun of Jesus. Ask, "Why did they place a crown of thorns on his head? Did they think Jesus royalty? Introduce the word *royalty*. Show pictures of kings and queens wearing crowns. Ask, "What did the sign above Jesus' head on the cross say?" Have children compare Jesus to royalty.

2. Ask, "What plants have thorns?" Show children an example of a rose stem or cactus with thorns. Tell children they will make a crown of thorns to remind them that Jesus is our King.

3. Provide each child with a paper plate. Show them how to fold and cut out the center to form a crown.

4. Have children glue elbow macaroni to represent thorns.

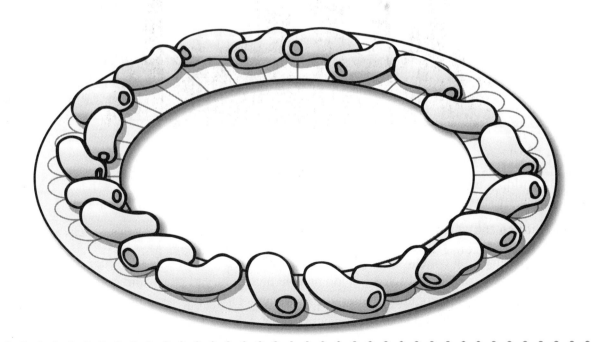

Jesus is Risen!

Matthew 27:57-66, Matthew 28:1-10

Jesus' body was placed in a tomb or cave in the cemetery. A huge rock was used to block the entrance to the cave, and Pilate placed guards around the tomb. Pilate did not want anyone to visit Jesus or take Jesus' body. On Sunday, Mary Magdalene and another Mary went to the tomb. The guards were gone, but the stone had been rolled aside. They looked inside but Jesus' body was gone! An angel told them, "Jesus is not here. He is risen!" The two Marys ran to tell the disciples what they had seen.

Teacher Notes:
Young children will have little experience with death and dying, so focus on the joy that the two Marys felt when they heard the good news that Jesus had gone to heaven. They can act out the scene.

Older children will have questions about death and burial customs. If possible, have a cemetery caretaker discuss his job or visit a cemetery to study and compare tombstones, dates, and epitaphs. Some historical cemeteries allow children to make rubbings of gravestones.

Marbleized Easter Eggs

Objectives:
- Children will use the technique of marbleizing paper with chalk to create Easter eggs.
- Children will learn that Easter eggs symbolize new life.

Materials: pastel-colored tag board squares, colored chalk, scissors, water in a shallow pan, egg templates, (page 92) pencils, hole punch, curling ribbon, decorated Easter eggs, tree branch or Easter egg tree

Preparation: Reproduce the egg patterns on page 92 and cut out to make egg templates to trace. Cover the tables with newspaper. Provide a pan of water at each table.

Procedure:

1. Have children recall the story of the stone rolled away from the tomb. Ask, "What happened on Easter morning? Where did Jesus go?" Explain that, because Jesus rose from death and went to a new life in heaven, we believe we will go to heaven also.

2. Tell children that Easter eggs are symbols of new life. Show samples of Easter eggs.

3. Demonstrate how to scrape the chalk with scissors to create a chalk film floating on top of the water. Allow several children to try this technique with different colors of chalk and then swirl the colors on top of the water with a pencil. (Do not stir so as to keep chalk on top of the water.)

4. Have each child choose a pastel colored square and clip a clothespin to his paper. Children hold the clothespin to carefully place their papers on top of the water. Remove paper quickly and repeat steps three and four as needed.

5. Children allow their papers to dry and then trace and cut out egg shapes. If desired, punch holes, thread ribbon, and hang the eggs on an Easter egg tree.

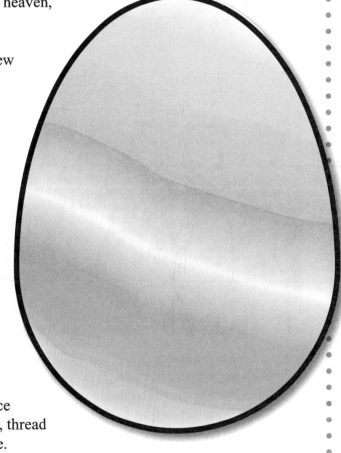

The Holy Spirit Comes to the Disciples

John 20:18-26; Acts 2:2-3

Jesus had promised the disciples that he would see them again in Galilee. After Mary discovered that Jesus' body was not in the tomb, the disciples were joyful, but confused and scared. They decided to meet in secret in a locked room. Although the doors were locked, Jesus appeared among them. Thomas could not believe it was really Jesus, but Jesus showed Thomas the wound in his side and the holes in his hands made by the nails on the cross.

Then Jesus blessed them, and a rush of wind entered the room. Flames appeared over each disciple's head. Jesus had left them with the Holy Spirit. We call this day Pentecost.

Teacher Notes:
Young children can dip their hands in tempera paint or finger paint to make handprints to remind them of the wounds in Jesus' hands.

Children will be intrigued by the story of Doubting Thomas. Ask older children why Thomas was doubtful and what would make them believe that Jesus was with them?

Chalk-Stenciled Pentecostal Doves

Objectives:

- Children will use a chalk technique to create images of flames to remind them of the Holy Spirit.

Materials: colored tag board or construction paper, white chalk, pencils, scissors, dove patterns on page 93

Preparation: Reproduce the dove patterns on page 93 and cut out from tag board to make templates. (For this project, we want to use the outside of the template — the relief.) Cover the tables with newspaper. Provide white chalk and tag board at each table.

Procedure:

1. Have children recall the story of Pentecost. Ask, "How did the disciples feel when they saw Jesus in the locked room? What would it take for us to believe today if Jesus came into our classroom? What happened when Jesus disappeared from the room?" Tell children that when the Holy Spirit came down it looked like a flame above each disciple.

2. Show them an illustration of this scene and remind them that the flame is a symbol of the Holy Spirit.

3. Demonstrate how to place the dove relief on colored paper and rub inward around the inside edge to outline the shape with white chalk. Use short inward strokes all around the inside edge.

4. Remove the template and blend chalk with fingers to make a ghostlike or ethereal image. Repeat several times to fill the paper if desired.

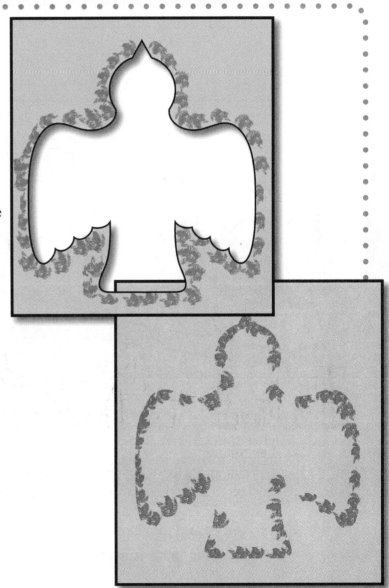

Make a Joyful Noise!

Psalm 150

The Psalms chapter in the Bible is like a songbook or hymnal that has been used for more than three thousand years by the Jews. Today we still have the words, but not the music. Psalm 150 is a fun psalm to act out because children get to make music! The psalm says to make a joyful noise with horns and drum, tambourine, violin, lyre or harp, trumpet, and cymbals.

Teacher Notes:
Young children love to move to music. Provide rhythm instruments such as shakers, drums, and bells so they can beat out the rhythms to recorded Gospel or folk music.

Older children should be able to use their listening skills to identify string, woodwind, brass, and percussion instruments in recorded music. They can create sound effects to accompany Psalm 150.

Shakers and Tambourines

Objectives:
- Children will create shakers and tambourines to accompany recorded music.
- Children will learn the word *psalm* and recall that Psalm 150 tells them to be joyful.

Materials: food coloring colors, bag of dried lima beans or navy beans, one clean, empty plastic water bottle with a screw top per child, one aluminum pie plate for each child, three jingle bells per child, curling ribbon, scissors, paper towels, shallow dishes or margarine tubs for each color of beans, Bible, musical instruments such as a drum, tambourine, violin, lyre or harp, trumpet, and cymbals or other available instruments, recorded version of "When the Saints Go Marching In" or your choice of hymn or favorite Gospel tune

Preparation: Cover the tables with newspaper. Color dried beans by soaking them for a few minutes in individual pans of colored water. Place beans on newspaper or paper towels to dry thoroughly overnight.

Procedure:
1. Introduce the word *psalm*. Explain that psalms are prayer songs that praise God.

2. Read Psalm 150 aloud. Ask children, "How does the psalm suggest we make a joyful noise?" Share some examples of musical instruments and allow children to explore them and make sounds.

3. Tell children they will be making shakers and tambourines to make a joyful noise. Provide a clean plastic water bottle for each child and have him fill it one-quarter to one-half full with beans. Screw on the top tightly to create a shaker.

4. Provide an aluminum pie plate for each child. Help each child string a length of curling ribbon through each of three bells. Punch three holes along the rim of the plate. Insert the end of the ribbon in the plate to tie each bell to his plate. Voilà! Shake your tambourines!

5. Play any recorded favorite hymn or Gospel tune, and have children play along with their rhythm instruments. Young children will enjoy marching around too.

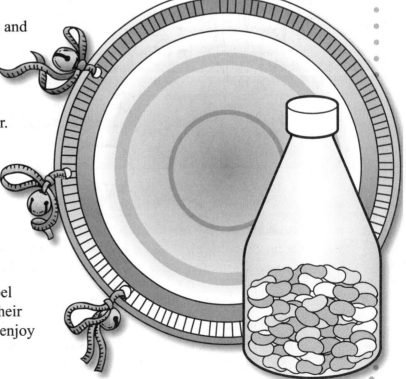

The Lord Is My Shepherd

Psalm 23

Psalm 23 is a favorite psalm for many Christians because it gives hope and strength in difficult times. It gives us images of sheep in green pastures, still waters, and serenity. It reminds us that Jesus gives us everything we need to be safe and happy.

Teacher Notes:
Children will understand the job of a shepherd is to keep his sheep safe. Young children can act out the sheep and shepherd. Provide props of a shepherd's staff and wooly hats.

In Green Pastures Finger Painting

Objectives:
- Children will use finger paints to create green pastures.
- Children will learn the word *psalm* and recall that Psalm 23 tells them that the Lord is our Shepherd.

Materials: green finger paint, plastic spoons, finger paint or other white glossy paper, glue, cotton balls, black marker, sponges, shallow pan of water

Preparation: Cover the tables with newspaper.

Procedure:

1. Introduce the word *psalm*. Explain that Psalm 23 is a prayer song that praises God for his goodness. Jesus is our Shepherd, and we are his sheep. Jesus keeps us safe and gives us what we need.

2. Introduce the word *pasture*. Ask, "What animals would you see in a pasture?" Tell children they will put wooly sheep in their pasture pictures.

3. Wet the entire front of each paper with a sponge. Place a spoonful of green finger paint on the paper.

4. Have children use their fingers to spread the paint all across the paper to create a green pasture.

5. Allow paintings to dry.

6. Next class time, have children glue cotton balls randomly in the green pasture and add legs with black marker to make sheep.

Serpent Pattern

Use with "A Coiled Serpent" on page 5.

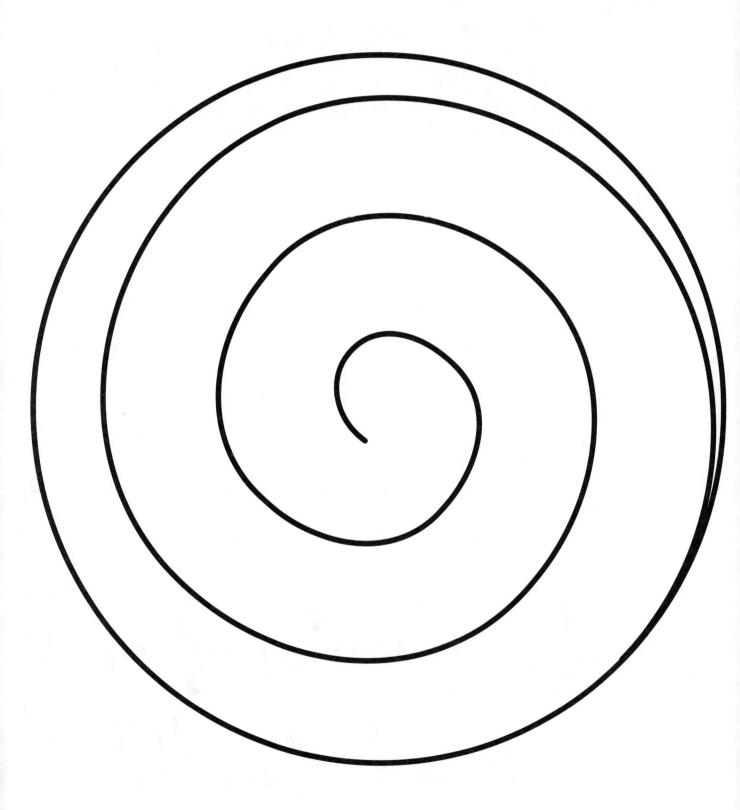

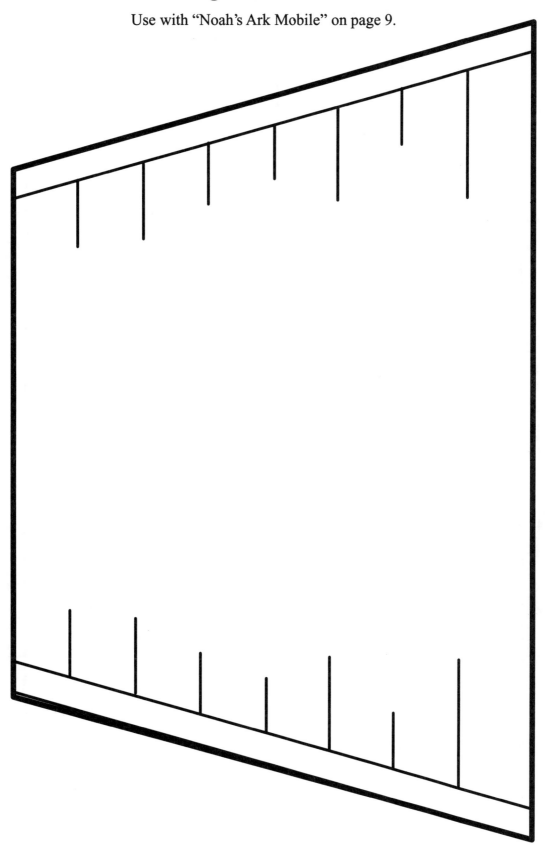

Noah's Ark Pattern

Use with "Noah's Ark Mobile" on page 9.

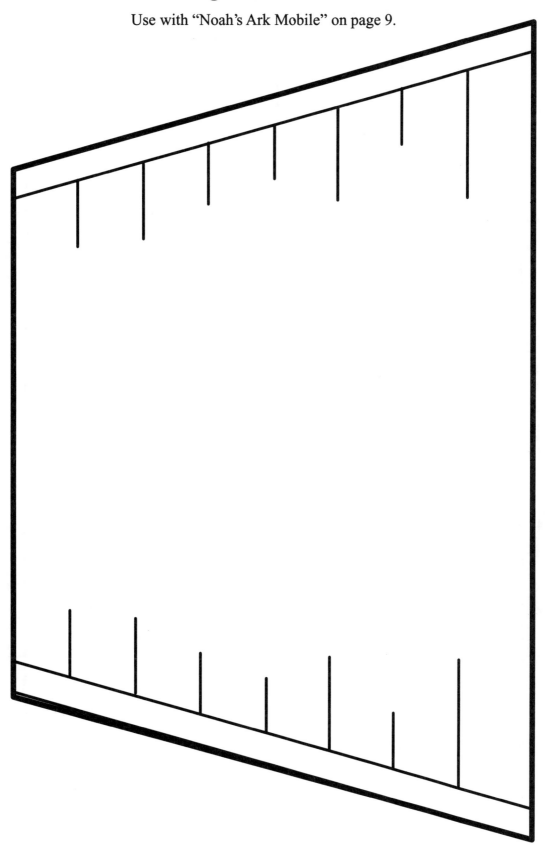

Joseph's Coat Patterns

Use with "Joseph's Robe Bag Puppet" on page 11.

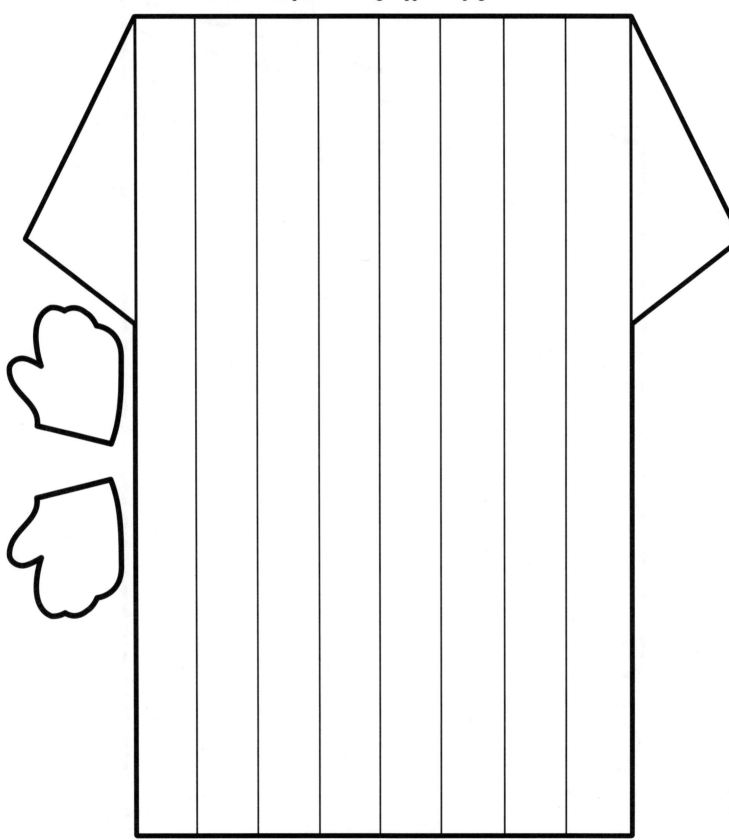

Frog Pattern

Use with "Frog Prints and Jumping Frogs" on page 19.

Jonah and the Whale Patterns

Use with "A Whale of a Tale" on page 35.

Lion Patterns

Use with "A Lion Mask" on page 33.

Have each child trace and cut out six yellow circles (3 ½ in. in diameter), one black circle (3 ½ in. in diameter), and two black circles (1 in. in diameter.) Children also trace and cut out two yellow ears.

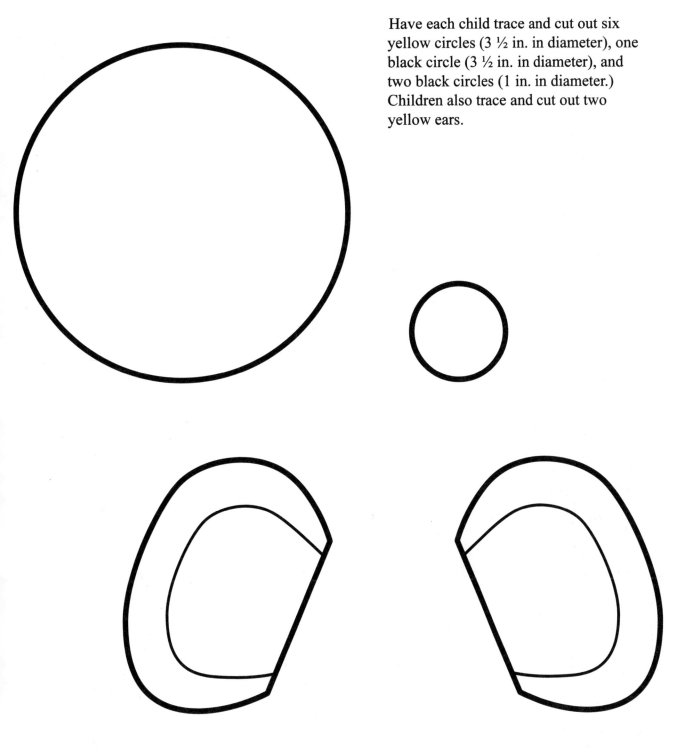

Donkey Patterns

Use with "Donkey Christmas Ornaments" on page 39.

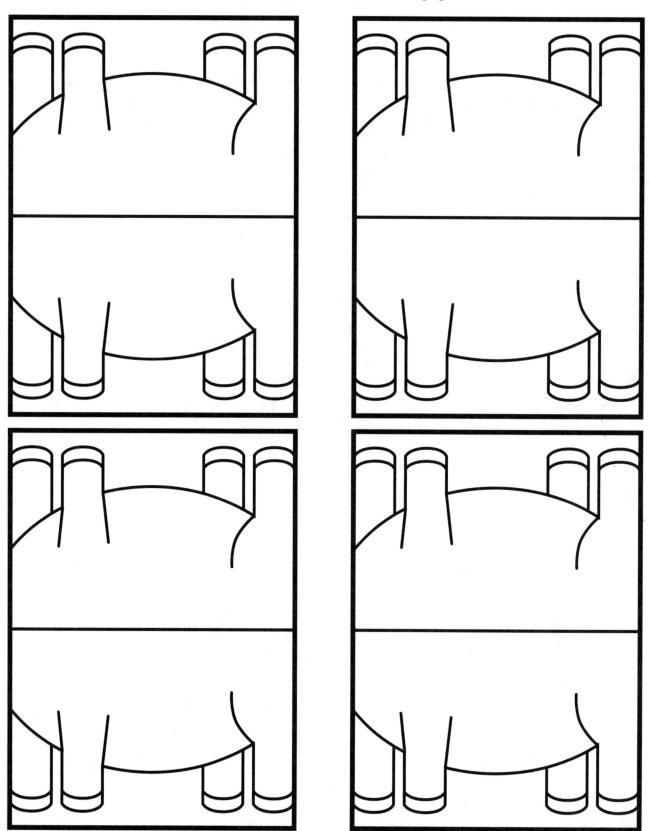

Camel Pattern

Use with "Follow the Star" on page 45.

Nativity Patterns

Use with "Baby in a Manger" on page 41.

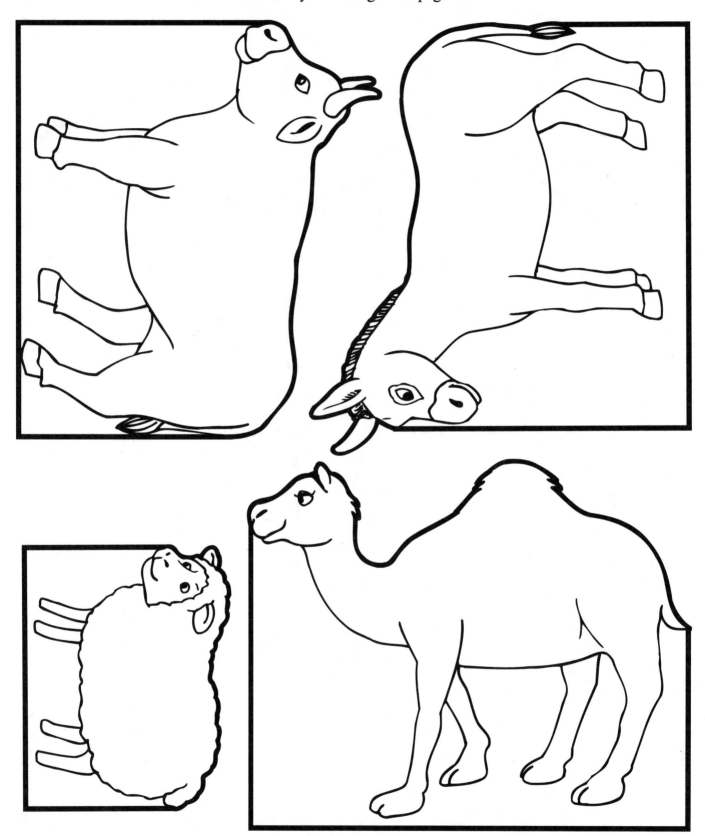

Fish Patterns

Use with "Fishes and Loaves Lunch Bag" on page 53.

Loaf Patterns

Use with "Fishes and Loaves Lunch Bag" on page 53.

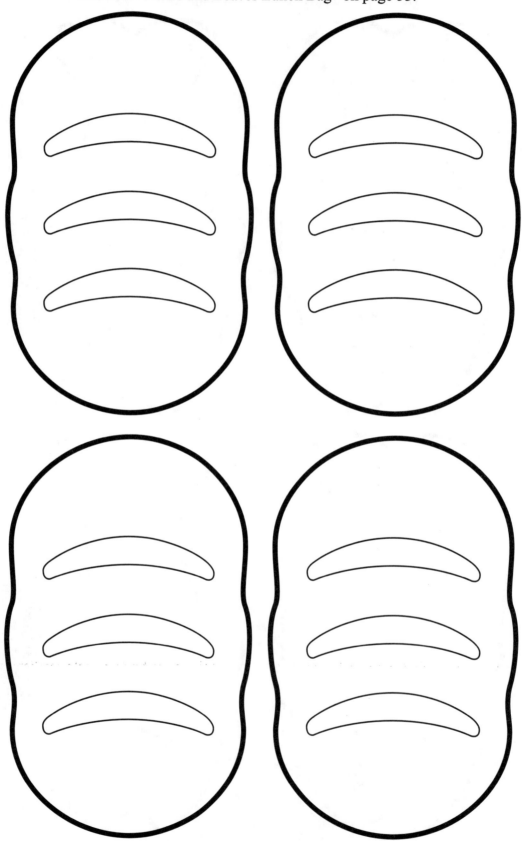

Sheep Patterns

Use with "Lost Sheep Stick Puppets" on page 61.

Rooster and Egg Patterns

Use with "Rooster at Sunrise" on page 69.

Use with "Marbleized Easter Eggs" on page 73.

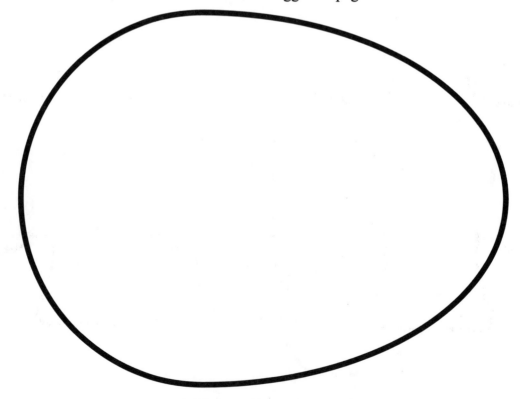

Dove Patterns

Use with "Holy Spirit Door Hanger" on page 49.

Arts and Crafts Recipes

Uncooked Play Dough

3 cups flour
1 ½ cups salt
¼ cup vegetable oil
1 cup water
1 T. food coloring (if desired)

In a large bowl, mix all ingredients together. Add 1 T. food coloring if desired. Store play dough in individual zippered plastic bags labeled with each child's name.

Cooked Play Dough
(That Bounces)

2 cups flour
1-2 T. cream of tartar
1 cup salt
¼ cup vegetable oil
1 cup water

Mix all ingredients in a large saucepan. Cook on medium heat, stirring constantly with a wooden spoon until the dough forms a ball. Remove from heat. Allow dough to cool then knead the dough till smooth. Store in a zippered plastic bag in the refrigerator.

Cornstarch Play Dough
(That Hardens)

2 cups cornstarch
1 cup baking soda
1 cup water

If desired, add food coloring to the water. Mix all ingredients in a large saucepan. Cook over low heat until a ball forms. Remove from heart and knead the dough with a wooden spoon as it cools. Store dough in a zippered plastic bag in the refrigerator. Creations made with this dough will harden overnight. To speed up the drying process, put items on a cookie sheet and place in a warm oven (200 degrees) with the heat turned off. Allow to cool completely before painting.

Smoother Play Dough

3 cups flour
½ cup oil
⅓ - ½ cup water
food coloring if desired

Add food coloring to the water if desired. Mix ingredients in a large bowl using just enough water to hold mixture together. Knead till smooth. Store dough in a zippered plastic bag in the refrigerator.

Oatmeal Play Dough

1 cup flour
2 cups oatmeal (rolled oats)
1 cup water

Mix oatmeal (not quick oats) and flour together. Gradually add 1 cup of water, mixing with your hands. This dough has a different texture. It hardens quickly and should be used immediately.

Cornstarch Finger Paint

½ cup boiling water
2 T. cornstarch
6 T. cold water

Bring water to boil. Dissolve cornstarch in 6 T. cold water. Add to boiling water, stirring constantly. Cook until glossy. Add food coloring.

Flour and Salt Finger Paint

2 cups flour
2 tsp. salt
3 cups cold water
2 cups hot water

In a saucepan, add salt to flour. Gradually add cold water. Beat with an electric mixer or egg beater until smooth. Add hot water and bring to a boil. Boil until glossy. Beat with spoon until smooth. Blend in a few drops of food coloring.

Tempera Finger Paint

powdered tempera paint
½ cup liquid starch **OR** ½ cup liquid dish detergent

Gradually add dry tempera paint to the liquid until you have achieved the desired consistency and color.